PROCESS DISCIPLINE

How to Maximize Profitability and Quality Through MANUFACTURING CONSISTENCY

NORMAN M. EDELSON & CAROLE L. BENNETT

QUALITY RESOURCES.
A Division of The Kraus Organization Limited
New York, New York

Most Quality Resources books are available at quantity discounts when purchased in bulk. For more information contact:

Special Sales Department
Quality Resources
A Division of the Kraus Organization Limited
902 Broadway   800-247-8519
New York, New York 10010   212-979-8600
www.qualityresources.com   E-mail: info@qualityresources.com

Copyright © 1998 Norman M. Edelson, Carole L. Bennett

Printed in the United States of America

02 01 00 99 98   10 9 8 7 6 5 4 3 2 1

∞

The paper used in this publication meets the minimum requirements of American National Standard for Information Sciences—Permanence of Paper for Printed Library Materials, ANSI Z39.48-1984.

ISBN 0-527-76345-4

Library of Congress Cataloging-in-Publication Data

Edelson, Norman M.
        Process discipline : how to maximize profitability and quality through manufacturing consistency / Norman M. Edelson, Carole L. Bennett.
                p.   cm.
        Includes index.
        ISBN 0-527-76345-4 (alk. paper)
        1. Production management.   2. Production control.
3. Manufacturing processes.   4. Quality control.   I. Bennett, Carole L.
II. Title.
TS155.E266   1998
658.5—dc21   98-22048
                                                                          CIP

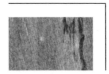 # CONTENTS

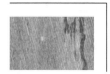 # LIST OF FIGURES

PREFACE

Even before it ships its first product, each factory begins to construct its own unique history and oral traditions. These tales, as told to successive generations of process engineers and line managers, typically include anecdotes of heroic successes, problems solved (and re-solved), 11th-hour solutions, and narrowly averted disasters.

It is the tendency to value heroic success more than we value the avoidance of the crisis in the first place that we deal with in this book. We believe that process upset should not be considered a natural part of the manufacturing environment. Here we teach ways to establish and maintain process discipline, to rationally anticipate the problems that confront us, and to circumvent the disorder and calamities that demand heroic effort to subdue.

Today's processes are usually complex, multivariable, multistep, and characterized by long time constants. They tend to be highly interactive; that is, any combination of moves — deliberate or not deliberate — potentially has much stronger consequences than historic data on single variables would predict.

Even minor changes in upstream processes, therefore, often have unanticipated significant impact on downstream processes and on product quality.

This emphasis on *problem prevention* is why we need process discipline, and how this book differs from its predecessors. The traditional tools and statistical techniques are still necessary, but they are no longer sufficient.

We are motivated to write this book because of our experience that process discipline improves and stabilizes production processes. The specific actions we advocate result in higher yields and fewer problems; furthermore, what problems do arise are of a lesser magnitude and more easily resolved. When we have achieved process discipline, our lives as managers and supervisors and team leaders and process operators are more tranquil and our sleep is more secure.

Our goal is to persuade our readers that assiduously following the methods and practices we describe is more than worth the effort. We include sufficient detail so that anyone can replicate the successes we have experienced by applying this methodology to a wide variety of processes and environments. We believe these methods apply to almost any process, and we include services and administrative processes.

Some of our readers may be working at small start-up companies just crossing the chasm between a few products lovingly constructed by designer-engineers working at a lab bench and millions of units manufactured in acre-large factories by newly hired production operators. Among our readers, too, are those who are old hands at traditional manufacturing but who have never lost hope that there is a better way to run the railroad. We trust many others will also find this material useful, and some of them such unlikely readers that we will not have anticipated their interest.

Throughout this book we attempt to identify the roadblocks that will be encountered and the hurdles that must be cleared. We offer pragmatic advice in how to move past such obstacles to achieve process discipline. We discuss the difficulties of maintaining process discipline after we have established it. This book's power lies in its authenticity and its practicality. We are confident that our instructions and strategy will enable readers to lead their own organizations to much higher profitability, and superior, more consistent product quality. What is more, the gains will be permanent and achieved at reduced levels of capital expenditures.

CHAPTER 1

THE GOAL OF NEAR-PERFECT CONSISTENCY

Introduction

In the early 1960s, as a newly arrived chief engineer of a plant making electronic capacitors, one of the authors inherited management of an unusual project. This program had generated tremendous enthusiasm among the optimistic visionaries, and had elicited derisive forecasts of doom from the practical real-world manufacturing types (like us). Our company had accepted U.S. Air Force funding to develop and demonstrate the capability of manufacturing millions of "high reliability" versions of our devices. These units, in the guidance and control systems of missiles carrying nuclear warheads, would be guaranteed to experience fewer than six failures in a million units during 1000 hours of operation. This was 20 years before the earliest mention of total quality management (TQM) or parts per million (ppm) quality specifications, and we all considered the goal unrealistic.

Nevertheless, we listened carefully as the customer experts explained and taught the systems and methods that government research indicated would achieve this impossible objective. We tried to establish the systems and procedures faithfully, and to execute them as nearly faultlessly as we could. We knew for certain that someday the roof would fall in. The customer would cancel our production contract before we could recover funds, and some unimaginably horrible accidents would occur. Our product would be known to be hundreds or thousands of times worse than guaranteed performance levels, and we would be vilified by the worldwide press. At that point, we would at least need to prove that we had followed instructions meticulously.

It did not turn out that way at all. Amazingly, the military's systematic improvement process and systems — the improved version of which we now call process discipline — worked. Our units passed a qualification test involving many thousands of parts at much more severe conditions than the specification required. We were the first of a gilt-edged list of component suppliers to qualify. The test was passed again repeatedly. Actual performance in field systems confirmed and exceeded what those test results indicated. And, contrary to the anecdotal negatives we sometimes hear, the product was highly profitable right from the start, and was that plant's profit leader for more than a generation afterward.

Just as surprising, we found (they had told us, but we had not believed it) that the exact same things we were doing to build high quality also gave us higher yields, lower costs, more predictable deliveries and customer service, higher output, and required less capital investment.

The results were astonishing, and because the methods were so straightforward and did not require special resources, we applied them to our most recalcitrant problems and richest opportunities. Some examples are:

- A plant bid for the contract to make a precision optical assembly of a kind it had never made previously, and won the job. Subsequently, they determined that the next two lowest bidders, experienced Japanese firms, had bid more than twice as much. The domestic plant soon learned why their competitors had been so cautious when they tested the performance of their assembly and found it failed for several important optical parameters. Financial losses and frustration mounted. Rather than retool the entire operation, corporate management appointed a manager skilled in process discipline. He trained and led the organization to run the operation in an extremely consistent, low variability mode. After months of steady progress, the performance specifications were achieved on a workaday basis, and the operation became profitable, stanching millions of dollars of annual losses.

- A new product line based on a proprietary coating was introduced and received strong consumer acceptance. However, the manufacturing startup of the new process in a new facility with new equipment was disastrous. After several months of operation, yields and uptime were stagnated at about 40%. Even worse, an expensive rework operation, requiring shipment to another location, still did not provide adequate numbers to service the market. A team of seven people trained in process discipline was sent to the site. In four months, yields were at 70%. In three more months, yields and uptime were at 90%. Not long after, the team returned home. The local plant, which had been converted to an operation based on process discipline after observing the progress, was able to maintain 95% levels by itself, even with an influx of new products. The turnaround saved millions of dollars.

- The successes of process discipline were so apparent that it became official company policy.

At about this time, a long and difficult research and development (R&D) program came to fruition. It moved first into pilot operation and then transitioned to manufacturing over a period of 24–30 months. A comprehensive and determined effort was made to establish all the elements of process discipline in full measure in the pilot plant, and to maintain and expand them through the learning and changes that were incorporated during the manufacturing startup. This was an entirely new product servicing the telecommunications industry. This company had no market position in the current products serving the worldwide market, and was entering a field dominated by giant customers and giant suppliers, many of whom were desperately working to develop copycats to the new line. For a newcomer to break in, it was vital to have products which performed to topmost quality levels as promised, to have manufacturing which consistently met its delivery commitments, and to be able to offer price/performance combinations which clearly exceeded current products. Process discipline has been recognized as the keystone of the manufacturing program that achieved these goals. The company's annual revenues on this product are now measured in billions of dollars, it is the world leader in market share, and the business is quite profitable. This business has received the Baldrige Award, the highest quality award given by the U.S. Department of Commerce to only a few firms each year.

We learned some things from this experience. These methods work. They make your organization wealthy. They elicit a skeptical response when initially proposed. In time, we also learned that the benefits are not permanent without continued strong emphasis on the key systems. Process discipline is not self-sustaining without management support and attention (except for those situations where operators themselves have taken ownership of the systems and refuse to function in any other way).

The authors and their associates have now applied process discipline — expanded, sequenced, and computerized to be more cost-oriented and less bureaucratic than the military original — to a wide assortment of manufacturing situations:

- startup of a new plant,

- move of a process to a new or existing plant in a different location,

- bringing new products and processes from R&D into production,
- improving yields, rates and/or quality in an existing plant;
- expansion of a new or existing process,
- manufacture of discrete parts, as well as continuous process streams;
- applications in new and old factories,
- high technology automated operations, and manual ones;
- plants which made one product and those which made thousands,
- operations in many parts of the United States and plants in Australia, Brazil, China, Finland, France, Germany, Japan, Mexico, Poland, Russia, South Korea, Taiwan, and the United Kingdom, among others.

Process discipline has always worked. It has always exceeded whatever was being done previously, and it has exceeded whatever else was tried. It is simple and logical. It is based on two principles: USE WHAT YOU KNOW and PRESERVE WHAT YOU LEARN. First, every person in the operation should be *using* whatever the most knowledgeable and sophisticated people know about the process. Second, individuals must immediately capture and *preserve* and use and teach whatever new things they learn about the process.

If process discipline is so effective and simple, why has not everyone converted to it? The answer is that it requires two things that many people (management and workers both) resist: work and discipline. But many of us are willing to pay the cheap price of work and discipline. For us, the benefits of greatly enhanced yields, quality, output, competitive position, market share, customer service, and profit are worth it.

We authors want to give you readers the opportunity for success in return for work and discipline. We will provide the most straightforward description possible, so that by following step-by-step, you too can do it. Good luck!

Variability and Consistency in Manufacturing
How Consistent Are Your Current Operations?

> **"Process discipline is a combination of actions and rules which aims to achieve (perfect) consistency of successive iterations of the *process* to assure that each *product* manufactured is identical."**

It should be apparent from this definition that process discipline is a program to get consistency. Our ultimate objective is near-perfect consistency. In this book, we will show how near-perfect operational consistency leads to superb manufacturing results. Virtually all industrial manufacturing appears consistent to the casual observer, so why is this an important issue? Are not most manufacturing operations consistent?

First, both the Air Force research mentioned previously and the authors' experiences have taught us that it takes a lot of consistency to get manufacturing to perform outstandingly. The converse of this is that a little bit of inconsistency can be very destructive to good results. (All of us can think of just one operational characteristic in our own process that could make all the output bad *even if everything else were perfect*.) Just about everyone has heard the nostrum, "There is no such thing as a small change to the process." Another way of saying that is, "Any change to the process, *no matter how minor*, has the *potential* to make the output bad." If you accept the correlation between near-perfect consistency and superb manufacturing, and superb manufacturing is your goal, you need to be extremely consistent.

Let us take a more thorough look at your manufacturing consistency:

- Right after shift change, when a new crew takes over the line, does anyone ever make some "adjustments" to the process or equipment to make it run "better" or faster (or slower), or more to his or her liking?

- If one of your products was carefully inspected by all of the people who do this job, would one or more of them ever arrive at different decisions?

- Are there any operations in your process that do not have a clear written description of the correct way to do the job and which detail all the correct settings for each of the adjustable variables?

- Are there any operations in your process which do not get randomly audited by an independent knowledgeable person to assure the operation is being run strictly according to procedure?

- Do you ever have an operator performing a segment of your process who has not received prior training on the specific equipment and to the written procedure?

- Are there operations or situations where your operators, inspectors, or set-up or maintenance personnel do not get an opportunity to review the procedures they use and propose needed changes to them?

- Are there any operations in your process where the assigned personnel would not set them up or troubleshoot them in the same way?

- Are there ever any changes to the process which are instituted without supporting data either from experiments or from carefully gathered process data, or without approval from knowledgeable responsible personnel, or without training personnel on the change, or without a detailed schedule for implementation?

- Are there any experiments conducted on your process which do not have a detailed written proposal that is reviewed for randomization, adequate sample size, risk exposure, instrument calibration, and the logic to justify intended action?

There are still more questions we should ask about raw material variability, tooling accuracy, maintenance, process information accuracy and comprehensiveness, rework, packaging, labeling, etc. Every one of these items has a direct or potential impact on consistency.

Truthfully, there is a wide gap between all but the very best of our operations and near-perfect consistency. However, this gap is a measure of the improvability of the process, and it assures us of being able to make important and often lucrative enhancing changes to the process. The gap indicates the extent of the value we can add.

How Processes Become Variable: A Fable

Jamestown was an otherwise well run plant, but without process discipline. Jamestown started out 10 months ago with a four-step process: cutting, drilling, printing, and baking. There was one machine at each step, and each machine was operated by a single person. After four months, production was increased, and the same operation was then run for three shifts around the clock using 12 people.

Jamestown was a smart and progressive factory. Operators were carefully selected for intelligence, skill, creativity, and prior history of excellent attendance and interpersonal relations. The fine technical staff had developed its products and processes. They had also trained all the operators, not only in how to do the operations, but also on the reasons why operations were performed in a certain way, and what some of the still-questionable areas were. These carefully recruited operators were told that they were responsible for running the operation to meet production and quality goals, and for improving cost-effectiveness and competitiveness. Everyone anticipated success and prosperity.

As the weather turned warm, John (who worked the day shift at baking) found the heat objectionable, and opened all the doors and windows when he came on. Mary (who arrived at 4:00 P.M.) closed them in the evening when she got chilly. The midnight shift operator was not very concerned with temperature, and he mostly left the windows and doors as he found them, except when there was a thunderstorm.

Linda, a cutter, thought the material was too tough for good cutting. She contacted the supplier and had them send two special batches for her to test, one softer, and one with the reinforcing material more uniformly dispersed. Stan, another cutter, thought he could identify good cutting material when he saw it, and he just searched through the current stock, selecting those pieces he liked. Miwako was sure the way to improve cutting was with better blades, and she was "experimenting" with diamond blades with two different bonds.

Art, a driller, thought carbide drills would work much better than the high speed steel ones they were using, so he picked up a few at Wal-Mart and started using them. Patricia, another driller, arranged for maintenance to add a coolant circulation system, and was drilling the parts wet. She was planning to check out whether soluble oil or plain water worked best. Enrique, the third driller, felt the machine could turn out more parts as it was, and he increased the downfeed rate by 10%.

Esther, who worked at printing, learned that the ink cost $112 a gallon. She suspected that the cleaning solvent ($7 a gallon) could be used as an extender, and she started putting 5% of solvent in the ink container, after a trial on two parts by adding solvent with an eye dropper. Marty, another printer, noticed that the print was smearing and skipping sometimes. He thought the commercial printer was inadequate, and he convinced purchasing to order the latest high-tech printing head which had two microprocessors. It came in by FedEx, and was installed on a Sunday. It took six weeks to find and fix the new unit's sensitivity to static electricity. Omar speculated that the print problems were caused by the wet cut at drilling, which infuriated Patricia.

Management was proud of its innovative workforce — "best in the industry," as the plant manager often observed. Yield, quality, and delivery problems were occurring, but everyone knew they were typical of start up and rapid expansion. Management fully expected that all problems would be found and fixed as "shakedown" of the process proceeded. Because market demand was strong and output was lagging, they decided to add another line with four new machines that would also run three shifts.

They proudly announced that "each of the 12 new operators would be trained by the corresponding operator on the existing line, preserving process knowledge and maintaining the marvelous current spirit of innovation."

Epilogue: Things never got better. Problems only multiplied. Competitors outperformed and underpriced Jamestown. Management was replaced by the new owner's team. The new group soon realized that, although all the "innovative" moves were well-intentioned, they had severely weakened the operation. Furthermore, the culture of "no process discipline" had irreversibly permeated the plant. Jamestown was closed, and all its jobs were lost.

The introductory fable above may sound exaggerated to some, but those who have worked in plants know that insidious (operating in a slow or not easily apparent manner; more dangerous than seems evident) process modifications like these occur in even the best-managed places. Here are some of the common reasons why random eruptions of "spontaneous" process changes happen:

- The process was never fully defined and documented, so a large (infinite?) variety of alternatives fall within the operator's allowed actions.

- The operator was not thoroughly trained to the defined process.

- Employees have not been taught the requirement for careful scrutiny and test of all new ideas or potential process changes before they can be implemented.

- Management may actually support as innovative the concept of operators making "private small trials" of new ideas outside the formal system.

- The plant may not have established a culture of strict attention to detail, precise running by the numbers, a strong infrastructure of systems, and emphasis on consistent operation of the process. Another way of saying this is that the operation does not function in a process discipline environment.

■ These issues may apply to their suppliers and contractors.

This list consists mostly of actions *not* taken, limits *not* imposed, and preventive systems *not* established and maintained. It is natural for operations to become more variable and deteriorate with time. It takes actions, systems, training, communication, and management control to prevent the process from becoming more variable. It takes even more intervention to reverse the effect and make the process more consistent. This is where the work comes in.

The Journey From Variability to Consistency

Most plants worldwide, including those that have been operating successfully for years, exhibit many of the behaviors we saw in Jamestown. Some might say that Americans are particularly vulnerable to these issues, that it is traditional for Americans to pursue independent actions and innovations, to reject discipline and controls more than other national groups. Truthfully, there was a time when Americans accepted this (biased) view of the world without ever checking the hypothesis. But Americans have since been told (angrily and incorrectly) by the Germans and Japanese, "You can get Americans to obey your process discipline rules and limits, but our workers would never submit to them. They insist on their creative freedom, and their ability to adjust the process." We shook our heads in astonishment, and inserted the word "worldwide" as the third word in this paragraph.

Why do most plants, worldwide, exhibit Jamestown behaviors, and how can these factories be fixed so they can first survive, and then become quite profitable? These answers are now known.

It is quite unlikely that all the people in a plant will naturally perform all their repetitive tasks near-perfectly consistently. Human performance will vary for many reasons: desire to explore alternatives; desire to make the work simpler or easier; whether the operation is physically structured so that it is easy to do the operation the right way; how people are being compensated or evaluated; operator fatigue; and numerous other factors. However, in addition to human performance features, there are the issues of whether the equipment and tooling and instrumentation keep functioning in stable fashion, whether the raw materials remain consistent, and whether the surrounding environment and services remain stable (air pressure and purity, water pressure and purity, power, temperature, humidity, etc.).

Happily, you are not powerless in facing the prospect of all this potential and real variability. You can proactively apply the tools and principles of process discipline to first constrain the expansion of variability; then, you can apply and strengthen your systems to keep reducing the process variability that you started with. The application of process discipline takes you on a long journey from variability to consistency. The consistency that you can achieve is always imperfect, but it may be orders of magnitude better than the original. With good work and good judgment, it can be so effective that it puts you in a predominant position in the business. That is the goal, and process discipline can get you there.

Two other aspects of process discipline make it even more beneficial to apply. First, the systems built to implement process discipline are exactly the systems needed to maintain the operation at the high state of consistency you have worked to accomplish. Stated another way, as long as you keep implementing the systems already developed, you will not retrogress.

Second, one of the main advantages of process discipline is that it enables you to accomplish major (and minor) improvements without process upset. It assures that any upgrade will accomplish its objective, and will not incur any unforeseen troubles.

As process discipline is implemented, you can be assured that if you take your foot off the accelerator and stop active variability reduction, you will stay on cruise control and maintain the gains already achieved. Major changes and improvements will come in with a safety net to prevent unforeseen difficulties and assure the success of the change. These two benefits by themselves would be reason enough to pursue process discipline.

What Process Discipline Is and Is Not

What Process Discipline Is

"Process Discipline is a combination of actions and
rules which aims to achieve (perfect) consistency of
successive iterations of the *process* to assure that
each *product* manufactured is identical."

While this is a satisfactory definition, we will need to discuss in
more detail how to attain it and what its limits and boundaries are.

You can think of process discipline as the collection of all
those things you must do and all the rules you must follow to get
your manufacturing process to run with near-perfect consistency.
You can also think of a process discipline environment as a place
where people practice behaviors that are supportive of and con-
ducive to near-perfectly consistent manufacturing. (In this book,
we will use "perfect" only when referring to process discipline as
an ideal, as in the definition, and we will use "near-perfect" when
discussing things that relate to real plants, because very little in
the universe is perfectly consistent.)

Among other things, practicing all segments of a manufacturing operation with consistency requires stability of materials,
equipment, instrumentation and controls, information received
and transmitted, test and inspection, and (usually, most impor-
tantly) the way people perform their activities. This book address-
es each of these issues.

It is not easy to achieve consistency. High levels of skill, organization, communication, and shared values are required. Best
known methods have to be defined, and everyone has to be trained
in the correct procedures for his or her job. It takes a lot of work.

Each person must also understand the general plant rules
which support consistent operation (the process discipline environment), and be committed to living within these rules. The
requirements apply to all people in the manufacturing operation,
and their observance is increasingly important at each succeeding
higher level of responsibility in the factory.

Let us review some general systems characteristics of the process discipline environment:

1. The best-known production methods available are defined and documented, and all personnel are trained in the procedures required for their jobs. No activity is undertaken without appropriate training.

2. Periodic audits of the actual operation (for compliance to the documentation) are performed, and the existing procedures are also reviewed to make sure they are sensible and correct. Feedback and corrective action are part of both loops.

3. Process changes are only approved when persuasive test data are submitted which demonstrate that the change provides the desired beneficial effect, and test data also demonstrate that the change produces no other adverse consequences. Before the change can be implemented, documentation is updated and training is conducted.

4. Production reporting systems are in place which provide accurate and timely data that are specific enough to enable management to maintain and improve the process, and management acts on this information energetically.

5. Other key support systems (maintenance, calibration, statistical process control [SPC], quality assurance, etc.) are kept strong and are meticulously observed.

The aim of process discipline is to run manufacturing in as singular a fashion as possible — with minimal process and product variability. Process discipline is a structured, controlled method of manufacturing which attempts to incorporate all available operational process knowledge in procedures which detail the exact best known way to run the process. By following those procedures carefully, all the knowledge is used in day-to-day operation. Process discipline rejects improvisation, "close enough," alternate techniques, sloppiness or inattention to detail, and the "freedom" to run informal experiments or to "try" unapproved changes to the process. And process discipline requires the consensual acceptance of the rules of the process discipline environment by all personnel.

What Process Discipline Is Not

Process discipline is not an authoritarian or "top-down" system for controlling operators. Actually, it works better when the procedures embody information and recommendations from process operators, and best when operators are the document authors.

It is not usually necessary to force process discipline down the throats of those who run the process. Operating people are the ones who have the greatest stake in stability and predictability. They are often quickly blamed for breakdowns, missed production goals, and quality upsets; and, they are the ones under severe pressure to rapidly find and fix the causes of these mishaps. They recognize and welcome actions that prevent problems.

Process discipline's strict requirement for data and proof before change is not a means to stifle creativity. In the process discipline environment, ideas are welcomed and anyone can propose a change. Technical assistance is provided so that the initiator of the idea can devise a valid experiment which can evaluate the idea's merits.

The need for proof before implementation of change turns out not to be a barrier to speedy process improvement. Instead, it is a guarantor of both uninterrupted high quality and the most rapid way to improve the process (because time and energy are not wasted on missteps or their discovery, diagnosis, and correction).

The very best operations we have seen are those where the operators have ownership of process discipline's elements — documentation, change control, training, and audits. In these plants, operating people are frequently writers, auditors, and trainers. They are in the approval chain for changes. They have the information they need, and the systems to apply it effectively. They willingly take responsibility for the ongoing stability and success of manufacturing. They know that, in the long run, their jobs depend on it.

It may be helpful to compare and contrast process discipline with some other familiar process and quality programs such as total quality management (TQM), ISO 9000, Deming, and Juran:

1. Process discipline is more rigorous and scientific. There is more insistence on careful testing and proof of the efficacy of a changed or new process, and process discipline stresses the **necessity of proving** no other adverse effects before permitting implementation.

    For instance, ISO 9000 requires no testing or proof. Its only requirement is that documentation be changed to match the new process (a much looser requirement).

2. Process discipline is broader and more inclusive than the others, which primarily focus on traditional quality control issues. It deals with statistics-derived programs like SPC, design of experiments (DOE), and sampling, and considers them important. But it also includes maintenance, production information systems, calibration, materials management, standard operating procedures, change control, training, and other factory systems that enhance manufacturing stability.

3. Process discipline is more real-world factory oriented. Deming, for example, believed that standard operating procedures were unnecessary and even interfered with the operators' freedom to run the process based on their own skill and knowledge. (This, unfortunately, would allow 12 different operators performing a function to run 12 different parallel processes.)

    Dr. W. Edwards Deming frequently declared his opposition to any quantitative objectives or measures, an idealistic way of promoting the idea that quality should never be compromised for output or cost. This conflicts directly with the need for manufacturing predictability, and we know of no company worldwide that has adopted these constraints.

4. Process discipline is more process oriented. As previously indicated, many nonstatistical issues such as documentation, maintenance, production reporting systems, discrete versus continuous manufacturing, process dynamics (the other programs seem to assume a steady state world), and the appropriate sequence of actions for major process improvement projects are largely ignored by the other programs.

5. Process discipline is tougher and more disciplined in its requirement for justification data, and less reliant on "soft" activities such as celebratory events and public recognition of accomplishment.

Process discipline requires acceptance by all participants of the rules of the environment, and although every effort is extended to make that consensual, exceptions are not allowed. We know a company where not following the documented process procedures can result in swift discharge.

A Flow Chart for Process Improvement

A three-phase strategy for rapid and permanent process improvement was formulated by analysis of the most successful and efficient projects carried out by a sizable engineering group over a 10-year period. The group was part of a diversified multinational corporation, and was headed by one of the authors. The strategy is captured in a flow chart (See Figure 1.1) which shows its sequential nature.

This strategy has been used for more than a decade; has been published in several journals; is taught annually in universities in the United States and Europe; and has been used to train engineers, scientists, and production managers at many companies. It is straightforward, logical, and it has worked every time.

It differs from conventional approaches to process improvement in three major ways:

1. It emphasizes that first efforts should be focused on making the process as consistent as possible to reduce process variability. The strategy authorizes this activity *before* trying to solve individual problems.

Figure 1.1 Manufacturing Process Improvement Flow Chart

Manufacturing Process Improvement Flow Chart

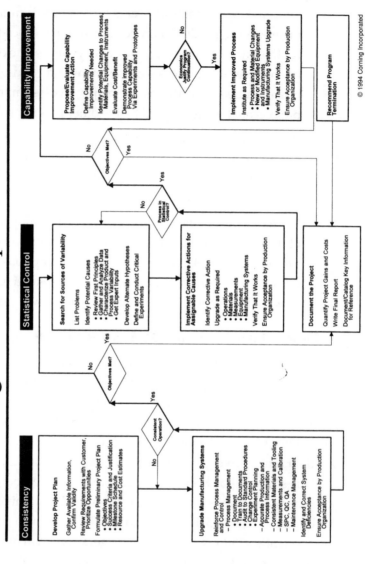

Consistency

Develop Project Plan

Gather Available Information, Confirm Validity

Review Requirements with Customer, Prioritize Opportunities

Formulate Preliminary Project Plan
• Objectives
• Success Criteria and Justification
• Milestone Schedule
• Resource and Cost Estimates

Upgrade Manufacturing Systems

Reinforce Process Management and Control
– Process Management
  • Document
  • Audit to Documents
  • Adhere to Standard Procedures
  • Change Control
  • Experiment Planning
– Accurate Production and Process Information
– Consistent Materials and Tooling
– Measurements and Calibration
– SPC, QC, QA
– Maintenance Management

Identify and Correct System Deficiencies

Ensure Acceptance by Production Organization

Statistical Control

Search for Sources of Variability

List Problems

Identify Potential Causes
• Review First Principles
• Gather and Analyze Data
  Characterize Product and
  Process Variability
• Get Expert Inputs

Develop Alternate Hypotheses

Define and Conduct Critical Experiments

Implement Corrective Actions for Assignable Causes

Identify Corrective Action

Upgrade as Required
• Operations
• Materials
• Measurements
• Equipment
• Manufacturing Systems

Verify That It Works

Ensure Acceptance by Production Organization

Document the Project

Quantify Project Gains and Costs

Write Final Report

Document/Catalog Key Information for Reference

Capability Improvement

Propose/Evaluate Capability Improvement Action

Define Capability Improvements Needed

Identify Potential Changes to Process, Materials, Equipment, Instruments

Evaluate Cost/Benefit

Demonstrate Improved Process Capability Via Experiments and Prototypes

Economics Justify Program Continuation?

Implement Improved Process

Institute as Required
• Process and Material Changes
• New or Modified Equipment and Instruments
• Manufacturing Systems Upgrade

Verify That It Works

Ensure Acceptance by Production Organization

Recommend Program Termination

Consistent Operation?
Objectives Met?
Process in Statistical Control?
Objectives Met?

Yes / No

2. The strategy indicates that this should be done by strengthening (or implementing) manufacturing systems such as process documentation, maintenance management, change control, production reporting, calibration, SPC, and others. In so doing, it integrates the use of a wide variety of tools and techniques of a stabilizing nature from many manufacturing disciplines.

3. The strategy provides a sequence of actions and priorities to be followed for most efficient improvement. Simplified, the sequence is to first achieve consistency of inputs to the process to reduce variability, second to identify and eliminate sources of variability in order to solve assignable cause problems and bring the process into statistical control, and third to improve fundamental process capability if that should be necessary.

The strategy, as embodied in the flow chart, tells in what sequence which segments of process discipline should be applied. The strategy is focused on fixing an existing manufacturing operation, but may be used with only a little flexing for startup of new operations, process development in the laboratory or pilot plant, and technology transfer.

Advantages of the Sequence

The sequence of actions to achieve (1) consistency, (2) statistical control, and (3) capability improvement, in that order, has important advantages:

First, many people can participate in the work to gain consistent inputs to the process. Writing procedures, training operators and inspectors, auditing the process, developing and collecting production and maintenance data, establishing calibration methods and schedules, and assembling limit samples are some of the activities required to build and enhance plant systems which assure consistency. There is a lot to do, but many people at all levels can contribute.

Compared to work on the second column (statistical control), and the third column (capability improvement), efforts on the first column (consistency) yield fast and efficient results. When an operation is standardized and documented and operators are trained in the procedure, many variables in that operation immediately become more stable. As a result of the variety of people who can participate and the benefits of standardization, column one (consistency) work has proven to be much faster in control (and yield and quality) improvement per unit time.

Column two activities fix only one or two variables at a time, and require systematic problem solving.

Action for capability improvement usually takes the longest to achieve tangible results. It generally requires capital appropriation approval, design, procurement, installation, debugging, and training before benefits are seen.

Making process inputs more consistent is "work intensive." It rarely requires capital or incurs risk; most often, it requires that all do what the most proficient are already doing.

Achieving statistical control is engineering or "skill intensive," and those skills are usually a scarce resource. Statistical control does not often incur risk or need capital.

The work on column three, capability improvement, is both skill and capital intensive, and is almost always the high risk alternative.

What are the consequences of using a different sequence? If you try to achieve statistical control with data analysis and experimentation before doing the consistency work, you quickly learn that (1) there is an endless list of process variations which must be hunted down and fixed on a one-by-one basis with scarce resources, (2) only the strongest effects tend to be visible through the high variability background, and (3) many of the problems you find, like untrained operators or insufficiently lubricated equipment, could have been easily prevented by column one actions.

If you attempt to go directly to the "new black box" column three solution, you see (1) without plant systems for documentation, training, audits, SPC, maintenance, calibration, change control, etc., even the best new process or equipment may function poorly or only for a short time before failing; or (2) the new equipment cannot cope with the high variability of material it receives; or (3) the problem could have been fixed more simply and cheaply by consistency or statistical control without capital investment and its long lead time.

It is sometimes difficult to convince plants with serious process problems that the vital first step is to operate with the discipline to run the process consistently. They want to immediately address specific problems. They feel that other approaches do not make sense. It takes a high degree of maturity and understanding for individuals to apply the strategy in times of high stress or crisis, and for the management to support it in order to get real, permanent solutions.

Data-Based Decision Making

The Inherent Uncertainty of Hypotheses

The human mind is incredibly adept at formulating hypotheses. Given a few facts, and adding a few surmises and perhaps a hazily remembered observation, all of us can concoct a scenario which "explains" something unexpected that happened. Furthermore, if you are told that the result was really opposite to what you had supposed, you could swiftly adjust your hypothesis so that it "explains" the opposite result. And, most agreeably, these hypotheses usually sound pretty good, and give you a warm feeling of satisfaction for having solved the puzzle.

Experience shows, however, that the ease of formulation is frequently inversely proportional to the accuracy and usefulness of such hypotheses when working on the manufacturing process. If you assemble even a small group of individuals considered experts in the process and ask them to review a "strange" result, you often hear a number of different hypotheses proposed and ardently defended. Logic suggests that only one (and sometimes none) of the hypotheses can be correct.

If you should ever act to change the process merely on the basis of hypotheses — even those agreed to by several of the most knowledgeable experts — you would be taking a high stakes gamble. This gamble will often fail *irrespective of the competence and experience of the experts*. The reason is that most manufacturing processes are complex and interactive. They depend on upstream occurrences and downstream consequences, on material and thermal effects, on variabilities in equipment and personnel performance. The combination of all of these variabilities and uncertainties makes the results unforeseeable.

In a real-life situation where the most knowledgeable experts were available through a dynamic and difficult manufacturing sequence, one of the authors tracked the hypotheses that were accepted as "probably true" over a six-month period. Fortunately, each was tested by careful experiment before implementation.

The results were that about half turned out to be correct, a quarter either had no effect or one that was too small to be significant, and a quarter had unforeseen adverse consequences. Several of the latter were so severe that all product in the line would have been wiped out, perhaps the customer would have been lost, and perhaps the associated financial reverses would have killed the business.

Some might say that these numbers were unusually bad. Our experience, however, is that in a reasonably complex manufacturing process, these results *are better than average*. People often act on hypotheses without careful follow-up to determine the results, and manage to stay blissfully unaware of the low success rate of such actions.

If process variability, uncertainty, and unknown interactions make the outcomes of changes to your manufacturing processes difficult to predict, what can you do to protect yourself? How can you be sure that the alternatives you choose and the changes you introduce (or are subject to) do not wound you mortally?

Data as an Antidote to Risk

Fortunately, there is a strategy you can follow which greatly reduces the risks that come with any modifications to the process or materials. This strategy can be simply stated: "Always require valid confirming data before making any change to the process, materials, or equipment." The data must assure you (confirm) that the benefit expected from the change really occurs, *and that there are no unforeseen adverse consequences.* The data must be valid (collected randomly and measured accurately) and have sufficient numbers that your confidence level can be high that the conclusions are correct and significant, and you must be sure the data cover all the important variables.

When you implement this strategy you embrace humility, objectivity, and logic as decision-making practices. You divest yourself of intuition, optimism, and experience as *decision-making practices.* You still use intuition, optimism, and experience *for formulating hypotheses, but not for decision-making.*

Humility is required because you must discount — actually try to erase — your own expectations, suppositions, and "knowledge of the process"; and you must be willing to let the data demonstrate the reality of the situation. Objectivity is necessary to be sure you eliminate all biases as you structure experiments and analyze the data from them. Logic must be your guide as you try to remove your own prior statements, your bosses' strongly held opinions; the cost, quality, and customer relations implications of the results; and any other "political" influences from your forthright interpretation of the data.

In some organizational cultures, it can be difficult indeed to maintain this pure scientific posture, but it is the one which guarantees the fastest progress in process and quality improvement (and in cost reduction as well).

It is generally easier to get agreement to require valid data to support a major modification to the process. It is often more difficult to get consensus to hold up implementation of somebody's "great idea" for a simple change until confirming data are available. Simple changes always appear to be free of risk, especially to the originator of the idea.

It is more important to require data for decision making on "small" changes, because there are so many more of them, because they are subject to the same uncertainties and unpredictability as more complicated ones, and because they often do not get the same degree of scrutiny and analysis.

So we believe the only reliable antidote to the inherent risks when process or materials changes are proposed is generating confirming valid data before implementation of the change.

The Correlation Between Proof and Survival

A basic tenet of process discipline is that proof from data is a prerequisite for process change or new process/product introduction. Process discipline supporters have observed many situations where seemingly attractive alternatives turned out to be serious mistakes.

Some other people (and companies) believe the requirement for proof before implementation is an unduly conservative and restrictive strategy. They often make changes based on judgment, experience, intuition, anecdotal history, or even analysis or simulation without valid confirming data on the manufacturing line.

However, probability theory teaches that repeated trials of even highly likely bets result in occasional losses. Experience with manufacturing processes demonstrates that the more complex the process, the less predictable the outcome of some change. But even the simplest processes and the most innocent seeming changes sometimes yield unexpected negative results.

Purchasers want to be able to *rely* on the performance of items they procure. They have high expectations of what they receive from vendors. They do not want units that merely pass incoming quality control or function satisfactorily at the first assembly test station. Indeed, they want to be able to *rely* on long-term performance of product buried in the ground or flying in aircraft, and even on promised deliveries and on competitive pricing. The general public has also grown to expect this.

Some years ago in Hawaii an airplane accident occurred where fatigue cracking of the fuselage caused the loss of several lives (although most passengers safely survived the landing). It turned out that this particular aircraft had experienced 85,000 takeoffs and landings. Nevertheless, a newspaper editorial asked, "What's wrong with American manufacturing?"

For a corporation or factory to survive and grow, it can experience only a minimum number of mistaken process choices. Sometimes, just one bad choice can be fatal. The more advanced and intricate its products, the more intimately related to human body processes, the more potentially dangerous the materials involved, the greater the likelihood that one mistake could end the organization's viability (not to mention loss of life and property). We all shudder at the prospect of faulty aircraft navigation or landing systems, contaminated innoculations, leakage of poisonous or explosive materials, or other potential consequences of process errors.

Viewed in this context, proof from valid data seems to be cheap insurance against wrong process moves. But, equally important, proof from data also provides protection against the much larger number of ineffective or adverse moves which may not threaten the viability of the organization, but which reduce the efficiency of operations, waste time and effort on diagnostic activity, and deliver lower quality product to customers. The result of requiring proof is more steady and rapid process improvement, fewer upsets and embarrassments, and greatly reduced risk of those fatal mistakes which would prevent you from surviving and prospering for many decades (the unstated goal of almost all organizations).

CHAPTER 2

PROCESS DISCIPLINE FUNDAMENTALS: OVERVIEW AND DOCUMENTATION

Overview

The five elements that comprise process discipline work together as a single organic system:

1. Document the best-known way to run the process.

2. Train people to operate the process as it is documented.

3. Audit to assure that you are indeed running the best way you know how and to provide feedback loops for corrective action.

4. Use change control as the mechanism to protect the process from the adverse consequences of unjustified change.

5. Require valid experimental data to justify the changes you make to the way you run the process.

The simplicity of the description belies the complexity of its achievement. Like other elegant systems, it can be attained only through an intimate understanding of the objectives to be achieved, the methods to be deployed, and a commitment to do it.

Here we describe what we have tested and found to work in real-life operations. There are surely different formats, different nomenclature, and different conventions than those we have adopted. We make no special argument for this particular configuration except for this: we know it works.

Documentation

Our concept of the organization of information to be presented in process documents originated before ISO, before the widespread use of computers, and before the age of worker empowerment. Whole afternoons in workshops with cross-sectional representation from factory personnel have been dedicated to discussions of the amount of information to be included, the order in which it should appear, and whether illustrations should be carried within the body of the text.

In the end what matters most is that the information be easily retrievable by those who interact with the process after they undergo a simple introductory training session to expose the logical structure the documentation follows. In other words, so long as it is consistent, clear, and complete we are all set. The devil, of course, is in the details!

Five types of documents are required for a complete description of the process (see Figure 2.1):

- Flow charts (process maps)
- Material specifications
- Machine (equipment) specifications
- Process operations
- Inspection/test procedures

Process maps or flow charts outline the operations, inspections (decision making about whether or not the parts or products flow to the next step of the process) and storage points. Materials that become part of the process or cause the product to undergo physical or chemical changes must be documented so that you carefully acknowledge any decision you make to change the

Figure 2.1 Process Documentation Summary Sheet

PROCESS DOCUMENTATION				
FLOW CHART (PROCESS MAP)	MATERIAL SPECIFICATION	MACHINE SPECIFICATION	STANDARD OPERATING PROCEDURE	INSPECTION PROCEDURE
1. Major Operations	1. Description	1. Purpose	1. Purpose	1. Purpose
2. Inspections	2. Suppliers	2. Equipment	2. Equipment	2. Equipment
3. Rework Loops	3. Specification	3. Materials	3. Materials	3. Materials
4. Storage Points	4. Incoming Inspection	4. Setup	4. Setup	4. Setup
	5. Usage	5. Operation	5. Operation	5. Operation
	6. Special Info	6. Maintenance	6. Maintenance	6. Maintenance
	7. Miscellaneous	7. Shutdown	7. Shutdown	7. Shutdown
		8. Safety	8. Safety	8. Safety
		9. Trouble-Shooting	9. Trouble-Shooting	9. Trouble-Shooting
		10. Spart Parts	10. Spart Parts	10. Spart Parts
		11. Illustrations	11. Illustrations	11. Illustrations
		12. Checklist	12. Checklist	12. Checklist

PROCESS DOCUMENTATION

FLOW CHART / PROCESS MAP — Write a Flow Chart for each product (or family of products) manufactured. Define both the product (including a Customer Specification) and the processes used to make it.

MATERIAL SPECIFICATION — Write a Mat'l Spec for each material required to make the final product, materials that comprise the final product, and materials required for the manufacturing operation and its maintenance. Generally, materials are consumable.

EQUIPMENT SPECIFICATION — Write an Equip Spec for each piece of equipment used in the manufacturing operation, for all test equipment used in inspections, and for special facility equipment.These documents explain what the equipment is, its function, and its component parts.

STANDARD OPERATING PROCEDURE — Write an SOP for all operations, auxiliary operations, and any other process related to the manufacturing operation. Document the best known way to operate the process.

INSPECTION PROCEDURE — Write an insp Proc for each incoming inspection of purchased items, of ware-in-process, final inspection of the product, chemical analysis, and inspections of tooling or equipment parts. Include test methodology and accept/reject criteria.

process inputs. Machines or equipment used in processing the product, and the operations and inspections the product undergoes, are the remaining three types of documents.

As we discuss each of these five types in substantially more detail, it will be easy to see whether or not your particular operation might benefit from combining one or more types. As long as the information is consistent, clear, and complete, there is no reason to agonize over perceived needs to have one more type than we have mentioned here; or, for that matter, one less type. It is our belief that the five types we have outlined are the *minimum* amount of information that you will need to document in order to establish process discipline. If you elect to include other types of documents — say, for example, administrative procedures — you will not be the worse for it, since documentation which is current and correct can hardly detract from the quality of your operations.

Flow Charts or Process Maps

There are software packages that can help you with this step, but flow charts can also be easily accomplished with simple block diagrams. The point here is that process discipline is not dependent on the latest and greatest technology, although technology certainly can make the job easier. Most plants easily complete these documents within a week or so of deciding to create them.

If you have no established system for flow charting, simply start where the raw materials or component parts enter the process stream. Show the major operations, inspections (even if these are separate from the workflow itself), and all points where temporary work-in-process storage can or must occur. The three-column format provides visual confirmation of all primary operations, inspections, and storage points (see Figure 2.2).

Operations are those things you do which change the character of the ware. Changing the character of the ware means that physical or chemical differences occur to the product itself and such change is discernible.

The intent of having a specific column for *inspections* (tests) is so that you can identify where operators have the opportunity to determine whether or not the product ought to continue in the process stream. These inspections can — and often do — occur in conjunction with the operation itself. Nonetheless, we have found that specifically calling out inspections affords us visual cues when we use these flow charts in problem solving or training. And, after all, the reason you are documenting your processes in the first place is so that you have a written record to form the basis of training, change control, and process experimentation.

If an inspection results in a decision to move the product into a rework operation, that loop must also be indicated. If rework operations take place somewhere besides the normal production step, add a separate box to show where this happens and how the reworked product re-enters the process stream.

Perhaps it is not obvious that *storage points* deserve a separate column. Each storage point in a process, however, represents an opportunity for things to go awry: shelf life may be exceeded, contamination can occur from unexpected sources, identification tags can waft from the ware to the floor, or operators can pick an incorrect item from the shelf. That is why we use this specific form. If your operation has process mapping software, or if you have flow charts which are serving you well, it is quite likely those will suffice so long as you can easily distinguish operations, inspections/tests and storage points, and the format is not unnecessarily complex.

We have traditionally included product specifications together with flow charts in our documentation scheme. For each product family (i.e., group of products which share common workflows), there ought to be a formal specification which describes the product so that a judgment regarding conformance of outgoing ware can easily be made. If these specifications are already in place, then you will simply ensure that an accompanying flow chart is prepared for each. Otherwise, you will need to create product specifications.

Getting It Done—Summary

1. Start with raw materials and component parts. Show where each enters the operation.

2. Show the major operations, inspections, and storage points.

3. Indicate any rework loops.

4. Assemble the product specification numbers for each product family (and individual products).

5. Develop your process flow chart following the example in Figure 2.2.

Figure 2.2 Flow Chart/Flow Sheet Example

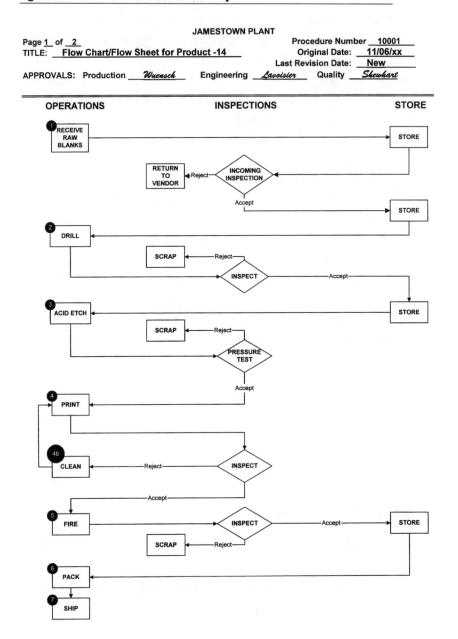

Figure 2.2 Flow Chart/Flow Sheet Example (Cont.)

JAMESTOWN PLANT

Page 2 of 2   Procedure Number   10001
TITLE: Flow Chart/Flow Sheet for Product -14   Original Date: 11/06/xx
                                                Last Revision Date: New
APPROVALS: Production   *Wuensch*   Engineering   *Lavoisier*   Quality   *Shewhart*

	Document #
1. Receive Raw Blanks 1a. Store in Raw Materials area until needed for production. 1b. Incoming inspection includes chemical analyses, unacceptable material must be returned to vendor using Material Return cards. 1c. After incoming inspection, acceptable material is returned to storage.	20001, 20002 50001
2. Drill 2a. Parts are drilled according to Product -14 hole pattern. 2b. Inspect, using template. 2c. Accepted material is returned to storage.	40001 50002
3. Acid Etch 3a. Parts are acid etched for fortification and hole deburr. 3b. Pressure test. 3c. Parts which pass the pressure test are moved immediately to Print department.	40235 50015
4. Print 4a. Print parts per schedule posted. 4b. After printing, parts are inspected and reject parts are cleaned and returned to Print. 4c. Acceptable parts are moved to Firing department.	41821 50237, 50348
5. Fire 5a. The 618-Abar furnace is used to fire Product -14. 5b. Inspection sorts those parts which have deformed during firing. 5c. Acceptable parts are moved to Storage to await customer orders.	42003 51688
6. Pack 6a. Parts are packed as 50's, 100's, or "Customs".	45318
7. Ship	45722

Material Specifications

Since the materials you use carry such potent possibilities to derail the process stream, contaminate your products, foul your equipment, and jeopardize your future profitability, it is no great wonder that we include them as critical to the process discipline mission. What is required is a precise definition of the material, its authorized source(s), and the methods by which you determine its suitability for introduction into the process. Materials are generally construed as consumables that require no maintenance, nor any troubleshooting.

Material specifications ought to include the following information:

1. A concise description of the material itself.

2. A list of the qualified suppliers of the material.

3. Specification of the material in terms of dimensions, physical condition, chemical composition, lot identification, material expiration date, or any other information pertinent to the agreement between your supplier(s) and yourselves.

4. Any incoming inspection which will be performed to ensure fitness for use in the process. If you are working dock-to-stock, then you will want to specify here that you will accept the incoming material as certified by your supplier to your pre-arranged specification.

5. Here you specify which operations or processes make use of this material. Materials Requirements Planning (MRP) systems refer to this as the *where-used* information.

6. If you are working with hazardous materials or materials that will require a Material Safety Data Sheet (MSDS), that information is included here. If the plant has an active program under a different aegis to ensure that MSDS records are filed and retrievable, then it is sufficient here to cross-reference the existing system.

7. If there is miscellaneous (but important) additional information, you can append it here as Section 7.

Operations which use sophisticated MRP systems likely already have formal material specifications. There is no need to create redundant systems if the information outlined above is retrievable and under some formal change control that meets the requirements outlined in Chapter 9.

Getting It Done—Summary

1. List each material that ultimately becomes part of the final product. Also list initial materials used in the process (at least all those that contact the product at any time during processing — materials such as solvents, chemical baths, packaging materials, and other potential sources of contaminants). Write a material specification for each of the materials on your list.

2. Begin with Section 1 and tell what the material is.

3. Continue by listing all qualified suppliers of the material. Include their name, address, telephone number, fax, and e-mail. This completes Section 2.

4. The specifications for the material comprise Section 3. Show dimensions, tolerances, physical condition, chemical composition, lot identification, material expiration date, and any other pertinent information.

5. In Section 4, identify the incoming inspections that will be performed and the decision criteria. Identify inspections to be performed by the supplier, and the data and any certificate of compliance which must be supplied (for dock-to-stock shipment).

6. In Section 5, identify all places where the material is used in the process, and (if required for clarification) indicate how it is used.

7. For hazardous materials or those that require a MSDS, include that information for Section 6. If the material requires special handling, storage, or disposal, include that information here.

8. Section 7 is for any miscellaneous information not yet covered. An example is differentiation of the usage of several versions of the same material (such as grit size, wall thickness, etc.).

Equipment Specifications

Equipment documents are different from process documents (which are covered in the following section) in that they are specific to the machine itself regardless of the type of product being processed. Another distinction is that these documents are used primarily by maintenance people, equipment engineers, and electricians rather than by process operators.

When a plant has the equipment specifications it requires as part of a well-established process discipline environment, these become source documents for setting up disaster recovery plans, annual shutdown plans, total productive maintenance (TPM) schedules, etc. Additionally, because they fall under change control, they act as an important communication device.

If a particular piece of equipment has been purchased from a machine vendor, then it is usually accompanied by a document packet of some sort. (Nowadays it might be a CD/ROM instead of a more traditional paper manual.) If the machine has been custom-built, however, it is possible that there are drawings or specification sheets, but little else in the way of documentation. Let us examine what is required in order to ensure that there is sufficient information to provide for training and successful maintenance.

You start out, as you do for all the documents you will write, by assuming that the document's users have the basic intelligence, educational background, and experience required to do the job in the first place. In the case of equipment specifications, you can address your document to machinists, journeymen, equipment engineers, and others who will install, repair, and maintain the equipment.

The 12 sections into which you sort the information for this type of document are the same 12 sections you will use later for process specifications and for inspection procedures. The content, however, is specific to this type of document.

1. PURPOSE

The intention here is to let the document user know what it is you are going to treat in this document. That is, why do you use this piece of equipment, what is its function, and what do you do with it. This section should simply answer the question "is this the document I'm looking for?" A single sentence is often sufficient.

If the machine is complex, it is useful to include additional explanation about the theory of operation. Keep in mind that a primary usage of documents you write is to train the people who work with your equipment and your processes. If you can think of information that will enlighten the user, include it.

The most common error in document writing occurs just here, in the purpose section. More often than not you pick up an equipment specification and discover that the author has elected to tell you that "the purpose of this document is to record what you know about [some piece of equipment]." You already know that is why you are writing the document! State the purpose of the *machine or equipment* you are documenting.

2. EQUIPMENT

There are three subsections required here. The first part includes information about the source of the equipment. The supplier's name, address, and service contact information are recorded in this section so it is easy to find when you need it.

Next, if the equipment requires auxiliary machines or components to function correctly, list such detail here. Include drawing numbers, suppliers, or other details which you think might be pertinent.

The third part of this section details the services required to keep the equipment running. These might include natural gas, reverse osmosis water supply, compressed air, liquid nitrogen, or a variety of other supplies. You will want to include any temperature, pressure, or flow information for each service. Think about what would be necessary to install this piece of equipment at another location and you will understand the depth and detail required.

3. MATERIALS

There are two kinds of materials that you will need to consider: materials that are used during the routine operation of the equipment, and materials that are used to maintain or repair it.

Operation materials include items such as slurries, solvents, lubricants, and the like. Since your emphasis in this type of document is on the machine rather than on the process, the information you are seeking here will affect the machine's ability to do what it is intended to do.

Maintenance materials are the oils, cleaning agents, degreasers, or other items that you use during preventive maintenance or repair or shutdown cycles. Include sufficient information to clearly identify acceptable types and grades of materials.

4. SETUP

Consider two conditions, and assign a subsection to each. First, record the conditions for initial installation of the equipment. This section might be as simple as documenting that the equipment must be installed by the supplier. Conversely, it might require serious depth in describing structural reinforcement, vibration isolation, city permits, or other special conditions. You will want to include sufficient information to successfully relocate the equipment elsewhere in your factory or at another site.

Second, describe the steps required to take the machine from a shutdown condition to full operation. This will include any warm-up requirements, initial setpoints, bootup of computer equipment, dummy loading to reach equilibrium, or other necessary drills before introducing product to the equipment. List the steps in sequence. If sequence is unimportant, say so.

5. OPERATION

Novice writers are sometimes confused as to what to include in the operation section of equipment specifications. It is easier than it appears to be, and this might turn out to be among the shorter sections. The confusion arises because of the temptation to include on-going process operation steps.

What you are looking for when you turn to this section is information regarding modes of operation: automatic, manual, semiautomatic, self-loading, etc. If the equipment in question runs automatically once setup has been completed, this section simply states that "machine runs automatically once setup has been completed."

Otherwise, include information about the switchover from one mode to another, automatic to manual, manual to automatic, and under what conditions to select which mode. Since you can assume that there will be a process specification for operators who are interacting with this equipment, concentrate here on the information those maintenance personnel or equipment engineers would need in order to return the machine to service following repair or shutdown.

6. MAINTENANCE

For equipment specifications, this section is the heart of the heart of the matter, for it is in proper maintenance of equipment that the factory has an opportunity to maximize its capital investment. Include here the recommended schedules and procedures for end-of-shift, daily, weekly, and periodic maintenance. Lubrication, parts replacement, calibration, and the like all have a place in this section.

You can choose some convenient and sensible way to organize the information in this section, taking into account the peculiarities of your own type of manufacture. A reasonable way, if you have no preference, is to organize it by frequency of maintenance, and that is what we show in our example outline.

7. SHUTDOWN

This section is the other side of the startup coin. Include at least three levels of shutdown information, beginning with what we would have people do to shut down the equipment during an emergency situation. Short-term shutdown and long-term shutdown are the other two subsections, and ought to be self-explanatory.

You may find that you want to include additional levels, and you should feel free to do so. We recommend, though, that you present them in order of length of shutdown, proceeding from shortest to longest. Include what steps to take, in what sequence to take them, and how to verify that they have been done correctly.

8. SAFETY

Include lockout/tagout information, safety equipment to wear or have nearby, and any special precautions for working in, on, or around the equipment. The appropriate level of detail is whatever it takes to ensure that plant personnel are as safe as possible. Organize the information in ascending order of detail, starting with the minimum requirements for anyone working on or near the equipment.

9. TROUBLE-SHOOTING

The problems described in Section 9 present themselves as equipment malfunctions rather than process or product conditions. We record the symptom (problem description), what might have caused it (probable cause), the things we can check to verify the root cause, and the corrective action which will get us back on track again. Word processing makes it easy to create columns for presenting the information in an easy-to-read-and-follow format, and we recommend you adopt it.

It is likely to be the problems you encounter which result in new learning about your equipment, and the trouble-shooting section of equipment specifications affords you your ripest opportunity to preserve what you learn.

10. SPARE PARTS

This is a simple but important section to complete. Make a list (if one is not included in the documentation which accompanied the equipment) of spare parts to be kept on hand. If you are including modules of replacement in your maintenance management program, then you will want to identify those here in Section 10.

Resist the temptation to catalog the component parts of the equipment itself, since most of them do not qualify as spare parts, but rather as replacement parts. The intention here is to have ready access to part number, model number, size, catalog number, etc., as well as the number we want to keep on hand.

Larger plants have whole departments to track and maintain spares. This section of the equipment specification serves as a source document for such groups.

11. ILLUSTRATIONS

Drawings, schematics, electrical diagrams, and the like make equipment specifications more meaningful and easier to follow. Include whatever illustrations you think would be helpful to document users.

Elsewhere we talk about linking scanned-in illustrations to text files, and we strongly recommend this technique wherever it is possible. If you do not have in-house capability, it is quite inexpensive to have it done externally through special service providers. Remember the ancient adage that a single picture is worth a thousand words.

12. CHECKLIST

Your checklist ought to include startup, shutdown, and maintenance. Each checklist includes the steps (the *whats*), in the proper sequence, without the *how to* details of the specific section. Many checklists require less than a single page, while others cover more complex equipment and are somewhat longer.

Getting It Done—Summary

1. The first section is purpose. It should be one or two sentences that describe what the equipment does. "The 716 drill press is used to drill holes in the perimeter of the flange holding the base."

2. Section 2 shows 1) the supplier's name, address, and service contact information; 2) other machines or components required for this equipment to function with drawing numbers and suppliers; and 3) services required (voltage, air pressure, etc.).

3. Section 3, materials, requires you to identify two kinds of materials: 1) those used in routine operation (slurries, solvents, etc.), and 2) those used in maintenance and repair (greases, cleaning agents, etc.). Specify type, size, quality, and give supplier detail.

4. Section 4, setup, has two subsections: Section A describes how the equipment should be moved in, installed, connected, aligned, and function the first time (and later, if it is moved). Include permits, licenses, etc. Section B describes how the equipment is brought from shutdown to successful operation and includes startup, warm-up, calibration, and how to determine the equipment is working correctly.

5. Section 5, operation, tells how to make the machine go through its paces and does not include anything about running the process. How to make it index one position, how to make it index automatically, and starting and stopping are typical issues covered.

6. Section 6 is maintenance. Specify daily, weekly, and monthly or annual maintenance, and parts replacement. If necessary, include procedures for major repairs.

7. Section 7 is shutdown. This section focuses on what to do for emergency, weekly, and long-term shutdown.

8. Section 8, safety, involves protection of life, limb, and company assets. Include lockout/tagout information, safety equipment to wear or have available, and special cautions and warnings.

9. Section 9, trouble-shooting, focuses on equipment malfunction. Record symptoms, what to check, and suggested corrective action. Be sure to add to this section new information learned about equipment problems when the fix has been completed.

10. Section 10, spare parts, is a list of those items that are necessary to keep at-the-ready for quick replacement. List how many of each should be kept on hand.

11. Section 11, illustrations, includes drawings, schematics, wiring diagrams, etc.

12. Section 12 is a brief checklist that includes basics of start-up, shutdown, and maintenance of the equipment. It should normally be less than one page.

Process Specifications (Standard Operating Procedures—SOPs)

The documents detailing how to perform the day-to-day operations that produce the products you sell ought to be straightforward and easy to understand. They will become your scripts for designing training programs, and they represent the current state of your knowledge about the process.

In competitive industries, we have encountered the argument that the very act of writing down how we perform our operations puts us at risk of our rivals discovering the trade secrets we use in manufacture. We are here to assure you that oral tradition in training your shop floor personnel and responding to process problems poses a much greater threat to your ability to compete than does the act of documenting your best known method of operation. Consider the consequences of word-of-mouth training (relying solely on the memory and ability of the trainer);

contemplate total dependence on a few key people to solve the problems which inevitably occur during the middle of the night or over the holiday weekend; imagine what might happen if your process expert decides to hold out for double the raise you think he or she deserves.

We once received an emergency call from a factory that had scoffed at our previous attempts to persuade them to document the processes they ran which relied on senior experienced operators. "Who needs documents?" they had asked us. "Our people have been performing these operations for decades and we have not hired anyone new for several years." The factory was 24 years old, and had initially hired a cohort of operators who were due to retire en masse the following year. They were going to lose more than three-quarters of their experienced operators in a single month. Now they were wondering how quickly we could help them document these processes.

Our purpose in recording the best-known way of operating the process is so that we have a basis on which to train new operators in consistent operation, to provide a common concept describing what we understand our operations to be, and to record new things we learn about the process.

We define the "best-known" way of operating the process as the method we use which consistently produces the most ware at the highest yields. Sometimes this is a highly controversial thing to establish, with several sponsors of contending methods. Here is your first clue of the benefits you can derive from documentation.

If there is no consensus among engineers, department managers, operators, and others, it is almost certain that there is rampant inconsistency in the way the process is being run today. While it may be difficult to settle on a single way, it is necessary to find a starting place from which you can launch systematic improvements. Pick one way and move on.

Process specifications follow the same 12-section format as equipment specifications, although the content of specific sections is somewhat different.

1. PURPOSE

Here we require a brief and concise explanation of why this operation (the subject of the document) is necessary in order to produce the product. You can supply a simple narrative paragraph, or you can include additional information.

At a minimum, describe which products must undergo this operation, and why it is necessary that they do so. Tell what exactly is accomplished through the operation, and consider including how the product differs before and after the operation.

2. EQUIPMENT

List the equipment required to perform the operation, and include enough information to permit positive identification. There is an opportunity here to cross-reference the appropriate equipment specifications, if such exists.

Include also gauges, microscopes, or other equipment, which require calibration or trouble-shooting. Any special facility requirements, such as air/gas hookups, temperature or humidity controls, compressed air supplies, or other characteristics of the work area which are critical to process or product quality ought to be detailed in this section.

3. MATERIALS

Sometimes it is not clear if a given item ought to be included under this section as material or under the preceding section as equipment. The determinant characteristic is consumability: if the item requires no maintenance or trouble-shooting and is replaced regularly, it belongs in this section. Saw blades, for example, ought to be considered process materials because they are consumed (and routinely replaced) during the operation.

Section 2 and Section 3 in combination ought to include sufficient information to completely equip a workstation.

If computers are used to record data, track process information (statistical process control charts, for example), or supply MRP information, be sure to establish a subsection for showing the system requirements and which programs must be accessed.

4. SETUP

Whatever it takes to set up the workstation at the beginning of the shift or workday belongs in this section. You can assume that the equipment itself has been properly installed, and that the facility requirements for plumbing, electricity, and similar needs are in place (for if this is not the case then you surely cannot operate the process at all).

List the steps in sequence, and indicate if there are some steps that can be carried out concurrently. Start with equipment setup, including any warm-up times or initial tests of equipment readiness.

Next, list any workstation preparations that are required. Filling out paperwork, collecting supplies, checking kanbans, etc. can be included. If there is any computer setup required, it belongs in this subsection.

The third subsection covers any·personal preparations that the operator must perform; putting on, for example, gloves or washing hands.

Job changeovers are to be detailed in the fourth subsection.

5. OPERATION

This section picks up where setup leaves off. Here we include the details of how to perform the operation, and this is the meat of the SOP. Step by step, you will record in sequence what is to be done and how you do it.

Recall that what you include here forms the basis for your understanding of what the process is. It will require specific approval to change, and you will train all shop floor personnel to perform the operation as documented. You will refer to this particular section of the document when you analyze problems or try to determine how to improve the process. It is imperative that you include sufficient detail, with sufficient clarity, to permit you to use the information appropriately.

Tables or matrices work well to define the process parameters under which you carry out the operation of the process. If several kinds of product go through this particular operation, then you can conveniently show the allowable range and desired nominal setpoints for each process parameter.

If there is a specified control strategy to be used, document it in this section. If you have defined desired responses to SPC information that show process drift or out of control conditions, then you must include it here.

Routine monitoring, checking, adjusting, and other process activities are detailed as well. If it is important for the process operator to carry out the activity, then it is important to document it.

6. MAINTENANCE

End-of-shift, daily, or weekly maintenance that is performed by the process operator belongs in this section. The distinguishing characteristic of the information to be included is that it is related to keeping the process up and running. Typically included are replenishment of process solutions, dressing of cutting tools, changing screens or filters, replacing batteries, stirring baths or dips, etc.

Time intervals ought to dictate the grouping of information. In other words, consider a subsection for each end-of-shift, end-of-workday, or end-of-week maintenance category. You might think of others necessary for your processes. By all means, include them.

Certain events might trigger the need for maintenance, while other maintenance items are performed on an elapsed-time basis. Group the information however you think it makes the most sense, but remember to be thorough and clear.

7. SHUTDOWN

Some operations run during a single shift, and others are more or less continuous in nature. This section can follow our previous recommendations for similar situations: use a time-based method for grouping information. Use subsections to delineate between end-of-shift, end-of-day, or end-of-week shutdown, and do not forget to include end-of-job changeovers.

Think of shutdown as a reversing of startup and review that section for clues as to what to return to storage, empty or clean, cover, remove, or disconnect.

8. SAFETY

If your facility has a safety officer assigned to maintaining safe work practices, enlist help from that quarter in establishing a protocol for what to include in your SOP's safety section.

If yours is a new plant or if you are too small to have a specific safety department, you can obtain a list of candidates for inclusion from your industry's board of standards or from the Occupational Safety and Health Association (OSHA) in your state. Here are some typical cautions to consider.

- acids and caustic substances,
- burns from either very hot or very cold substances (including certain sprays),
- cuts from sharp corners, edges, or blades,
- decibel levels in noisy environments,
- electrical shock hazards,
- explosives,
- flammables or combustibles,
- flying ash or sparks,
- fumes,
- gas inhalation or leakage,
- high voltage,
- hot surfaces or liquids,
- irritants in chemicals or substances,
- laser light exposure,
- moving belts or moving parts,
- oily surfaces,
- pinch points on machinery,
- radiation hazards.

If there are (MSDSs) associated with the process materials in use for the operation being documented, include them in this section.

9. TROUBLE-SHOOTING

We recommend the same four-part format that is used for recording trouble-shooting for equipment specifications: problem, possible cause, checks, and corrective action. Use a separate subsection for each problem, and describe the problem from the point of view of the observer of said problem — usually the operator in this case. List the possible causes in order of descending probability, the most likely cause first. Then show the items to check and the corrective action to take if the cause can be identified.

In this document you treat the problems and solutions which can be effected by the operator. In many cases, then, the corrective action that the operator will take is to call for additional help (from maintenance personnel or engineers or others in the factory). *Do not include information that would cause the operator to take inappropriate actions.* If specialized skill is required for safety reasons, for example, say so in the document.

10. SPARE PARTS

Here provide the list of supplies, forms, machine parts, bulbs, blades, and other items that you would expect to find at the workstation in order to run the day-to-day operation. Some operations require nothing. Others require that you have on hand items such as extra fan belts, dressing stones, and other materials. Document what is needed.

Do not include machine spare parts unless it is expected that the operator will be the one to replace the parts. If maintenance personnel will perform the activity, include it in the equipment specification rather than here.

11. ILLUSTRATIONS

By including all of the illustrations in a single section, you avoid duplication and make it easier to find the pictures that enhance your understanding of other sections of the document. In fact, if illustrations are well constructed, it is possible to greatly reduce the requirement for narrative text in other sections of the document. See the equipment specification write-up on illustrations to refresh your memory relative to linking text and illustrations in computer-based documentation systems.

12. CHECKLISTS

Many operations lend themselves to inclusion of a job setup sheet, and here is where you can include such helpful information. Some plants refer to these checklists as "standards charts" or "guide data" rather than setup sheets. Regardless of the semantics, these invaluable documents include nominal setpoints and allowable ranges for process parameters. They also list critical process conditions (temperatures, for example) and tools and fixtures which are required for specific jobs.

In addition to the setup sheets, the second requirement for this section is that you list the sequential steps of the operation (the *what-to-dos*), absent the additional detail of the *how-tos*.

If you have computerized your documentation system, and process operators access their documents that way, then the checklists can comprise a higher-level document where the exploded view (or "drill-down detail," as some systems refer to it) includes the details of the other sections.

Getting It Done—Sumary

1. Section 1, purpose, describes why this operation is necessary to produce the product. "In the furnace operation, parts are sagged flat and then annealed to reduce residual stresses."

2. Section 2, equipment, identifies the specific equipment used to perform this operation as well as the services, tools, and gauges needed.

3. Section 3, materials, identifies the consumable materials used in the process, and computers and programs needed

to generate information or to record materials used or processed.

4. The setup in Section 4 describes how a properly installed workstation is started and brought to successful operation. It includes paperwork, computer readiness, and personal gear. Requirements for job changeover are also detailed.

5. Section 5, operation, details in step-by-step fashion what the operator does to make a good product. Tables for settings and adjustments for manufacture of different items are often included. A wide-ranging, complete description is needed to assure consistent replication.

6. Section 6, maintenance, describes only the maintenance the process operator performs. Hourly, end-of shift, end-of-week maintenance, and that which may be required to improve process results (cleaning silk screens, for example, or dressing a cutting blade) are the focus.

7. Section 7 should detail what emergency, short-term, and long-term shutdowns the operator is expected to perform, and how to do them.

8. For Section 8, safety, refer carefully to the chapter material to assure that all mentioned items are considered, and relevant ones are included. The plant safety officer should participate in writing this section of the document to be sure that all safety issues are adequately considered.

9. Section 9, trouble-shooting, should be structured in logical decision tree format with symptoms, possible causes, checks, and corrective actions. It is important to incorporate into the trouble-shooting section all new learning about the process so that this section becomes increasingly comprehensive and more accurate and useful.

10. Section 10, spare parts, should include those items normally replaced by the operator at the workstation.

11. In Section 11, illustrations, include pictures, diagrams, and drawings which explain or show things described elsewhere in the document.

12. Section 12, checklist, is a place to store job setup sheets which show standard setup parameters for the various items processed at this workstation. It also contains a brief summary of the major steps (in sequence) to perform this operation. Strive for conciseness and brevity.

Inspection Procedures

Increasingly, inspection procedures are embedded in the day-to-day process operations and are carried out by the same people who perform the standard operating procedures. If this is the case in your factory, then the inspection procedures which you call out here will be easy to write and small in scope. Otherwise, they constitute separate and special operations, although they follow the 12-section format of both equipment specifications and process specifications.

Take the case where your high-involvement workforce acts as both process operator and inspector. It is likely, then, that the inspection steps to determine whether or not the product ought to be moved on to the next processing operation are part and parcel of the regular SOP. There is no need to write a separate document.

If there is equipment involved — coordinate measuring machines, for example, or perhaps a separate inspection room with a controlled environment or laminar flow hoods — then we suggest you write an inspection procedure rather than a SOP. The reason for this is that you want to clearly recognize when you are making these decisions.

A simple test you can use to determine which type of procedure to write is to ask if there are more than 10 separate steps and/or if there is a separate piece of equipment (as opposed to materials or gauges) involved. If the answer to either question is "yes," then write an inspection procedure.

The content of the sections and subsections follows very closely with that of the process specification. The chief difference between the two types of documents is the purpose for which the procedures themselves are carried out.

1. PURPOSE

    The purpose includes why you are called upon to make a test of the goodness or suitability of the product. You want to describe the characteristic, property, or dimensions that you are inspecting and why that is deemed critical to your customers.

2. EQUIPMENT

    Same as for the process specification, except pay special attention to conditions for the inspection to occur: special lighting, microscope power settings, etc.

3. MATERIALS

    These are consumables, as in process specifications. They might include limit samples for comparison of acceptability, data entry forms, accept/reject tags, material review board stickers and the like.

4. SETUP

    Discuss preparation of test solutions, calibration of instruments or gauges, obtaining appropriate limit samples or comparison standards, etc. Other than these distinctions, the same rules apply as those for process specifications.

5. OPERATION

    If there is a matrix that can be used to show product standards and acceptance limits, then use it. Otherwise, detail as you see fit, following the process specifications format.

6. MAINTENANCE

    Not likely different from process specifications, except that refreshing of test solutions, re-calibration of gauges, cleaning surfaces, and the like ought to be considered.

7. SHUTDOWN

Returning limit samples or gauges to storage, and other activities associated with conclusion of the shift, the workday, or the week are to be included. Follow the time-interval format suggested for process specifications.

8. SAFETY

No different from process specifications in the items to be considered and included where appropriate.

9. TROUBLE-SHOOTING

Generally speaking, the problems relating to inspection procedures have to do with the ability of the operator or inspector to accurately determine whether or not the gauges, test devices, or other supporting instruments are in good repair. Follow the same format as for process specifications, and provide information regarding whom should be notified to provide guidance until the problem is resolved.

10. SPARE PARTS

As might be expected, there is no difference between what one would include here and what one would include in a process specification. The exact nature of the spare parts is more likely to be chart recording paper or inspection stamps, but otherwise they are the same.

11. ILLUSTRATIONS

No difference here either. Just remember to include any pictures that might prove useful in training or clarification of other sections.

12. CHECKLIST

No difference.

Getting It Done—Summary

1. Section 1 is purpose, a simple statement of what you are inspecting and why.

2. Section 2, equipment, identifies the specific equipment, tools and gauges, and services that are used in this inspection.

3. Section 3, materials, should list consumables, limit samples, data forms, stickers, stamps, and the like.

4. Section 4, setup, includes preparation of solutions or other test materials and calibration of test equipment. For sophisticated test equipment, details of start up, warm up, and confirmation of readiness should be included.

5. Section 5, operation, follows the same format as process specifications.

6. Section 6, maintenance, usually focuses on cleanliness, lighting, tool wear and checking, and specific needs of automated equipment.

7. Section 7, shutdown, considers emergency, short-term and long-term shutdowns. Any special considerations for shutdown of sophisticated equipment should also be included.

8. Section 8, safety, follows the same course as in process specifications.

9. Section 9, trouble-shooting, is often tied to the functioning of measurement equipment. In high-tech operations these may be sensitive and complex pieces of equipment that require outside experts for repair and calibration. Therefore, the problems may have a wide range of difficulty from the simplest on up. Follow the directions for process specifications as appropriate.

10. Section 10, spare parts, follows the guidelines for process specifications.

11. Section 11, illustrations, also follows the guidelines for process specifications.

12. Section 12, checklist, should be a simple sequential list of the most important steps. If applicable, tables or matrices of settings for individual items inspected should be included.

CHAPTER 3

PROCESS DISCIPLINE FUNDAMENTALS: TRAINING

Writing down the best-known way to run your processes is of little value unless you train all those who interact with the processes to adhere to the standard you have documented. Not only must you ensure that people know and understand the specific work instructions for the process operations within their area of responsibility, but you must also teach the methods you have established for change control, for experiments, and for checking that the process is being run to standard. There are, then, two types of training which must be accomplished: process discipline training (a comprehensive introduction to process discipline and its constituent elements) and process training (that is, the work instructions for a specific process operation).

Systems Orientation

Organizations that are beginning their journey toward process discipline will want to conduct general training sessions outlining what is going to happen, the proposed timetable, and the goals that have been established. During the implementation phase, all personnel who will be affected need to understand the purpose of process discipline, how it will benefit operations, and how they will be expected to work within the new boundaries.

We know from experience that these early introductory sessions are both an opportunity and a danger, for the messages they carry can act not only as stimulants to active participation, but also to resistance. Much depends on an accurate assessment of the participants' receptivity to the message, and this will differ greatly from one organization to the next, or even within various departments of an organization.

Credibility will be gained or lost in direct proportion to how well you convey the benefits of process discipline. When these sessions are focused on the good that will come from the work that must be done, and the candid need for input and participation from all levels, we have found that people readily absorb the information and can quickly engage in the process. Here are some of the topics to cover:

- consistency and what it means to your operations,
- benefits which come from decreasing variability, even if you have not yet optimized the process,
- how to access the documents (which might include training in online computer systems),
- how to initiate changes to the standard way you operate the process,
- what is required to conduct a process experiment,
- the role of audits in maintaining process discipline, and
- how to propose improvements in the system.

While this might seem to be a lot of ground to cover in an introductory session, it turns out to not be so difficult after all. What we are proposing is that you *introduce* these topics, supplying sufficient information in outline form so that participants in these sessions understand that they are expected to operate under process discipline and what resources exist to support them as they work within the system.

We strongly advocate the use of real-life examples from your own factory. Talk about the problems you are experiencing because of lack of process discipline, and be sure to include successes once you have experienced them. These anecdotes help build a relevant and powerful process discipline training.

Orientation sessions also provide a chance for feedback from participants either during or after the formal presentations. Be sure to encourage it. Such feedback ought to be welcomed since it offers you reliable information about how successful you are at establishing the environment that supports process discipline.

Even after process discipline is well established, there is still a need to conduct regular system orientations for newly hired employees who will interact in any way with the process, for those who have new job assignments, and for regular reinforcement of the principles you advocate. If you already have a program for training new members of your organization, then you need to add only a module for teaching the elements of process discipline. Otherwise, you can create a stand-alone program for routine administration.

Plants we have worked with have successfully used flip charts, overhead transparencies, videotapes, and handouts to conduct process discipline training. The medium in this case is much less significant than the message.

Do not shortchange process discipline training. You cannot expect people to operate under process discipline if you do not equip them with the information they need to understand what the system is, what is expected of them, and how to use the system for their own benefit.

Getting It Done

1. Set up classroom training to introduce everyone to process discipline basics:
   - consistency,
   - how to access documents,
   - the role of audits,

- why change control is vital to the organization's success,
- what is needed to conduct a process experiment.

2. Emphasize the need for everyone to participate.

3. Train all new people in process discipline.

4. Use real-life examples from your own factory to build credibility.

Process Training

Regardless of experience, all engineers, operators, inspectors, team leaders, production managers, and others who interact with the process require training to the one best way to operate the process once it has been established.

Traditionally, you conduct this process training as soon as you can agree on the one best way and have committed it to documentation. Since the operators themselves usually take an active role in helping you define and document your best process, it may seem redundant to conduct formal training for these same operators. Not surprisingly, though, if you neglect this important aspect of ensuring consistent operation, people will continue to do what they have been doing all along and you will soon discover that your documents do not reflect your true practices.

The nature of the training should be determined by the complexity of the process and the prior knowledge and experience of the operators.

In some instances, training can consist of a quick informal review of a document or a group of documents and acknowledgment of their completion. These cases occur when there is an easy consensus on the one best way, and documentation simply confirms it. The key here is to ensure that people know the documents are available and have easy access to both the documents and a change control process to add, delete, or change the information they contain.

More than likely, though, most of your operations will not be so easy. Nonetheless, there are many ancillary benefits that arise from this element of process discipline and your efforts in conducting high-quality training will undoubtedly pay off. In the typical case, the document has been derived after much discussion and some debate. Process training, then, always includes acknowledgment that you have arrived at what you believe to be the one best way to run the process.

Sometimes what you have decided as "the one best way" amounts to choosing among equally likely candidate processes. This is especially true where process experiments are prohibitively costly or feedback loops are long. In some cases you simply pick one from among the contenders. Your training ought to include the facts of your selection process and some assurance to the trainees that, by consistently running according to what you have documented, you will soon see *in actual results* whether or not you are correct. The preceding holds true if, and only if, every operator on every shift every day follows the documented procedure. This is a powerful argument for consistency, even for those who think you have not yet arrived at the *best-known* way.

Good training will also address the problems that you can predict will arise and the trouble-shooting procedures you have documented to overcome those problems. In addition, you must instruct how to access the documents (whether in file cabinets or binders or software, and how the information is organized and presented).

As with systems orientation, there are routine events that ought to trigger training. Each new document that is completed is one such event. Large-scale process changes (those with sufficient complexity to cause concern about consistency) need to be introduced through formal training, so that problems are reduced and the change is smoothly implemented. Personnel turnover certainly warrants attention to how transfers-in will learn to operate the processes for which they are responsible. For operations that have intermittent processes that start up once or twice a year (or sometimes even less frequently!), training sessions to review the documents are required.

Most plants that are successful in establishing and maintaining process discipline understand that training is a cornerstone of consistent operations. This includes routine retraining and reinforcement of prior training so workers know what they are supposed to do and how they are supposed to do it.

Getting It Done

1. Train engineers, operators, inspectors, team leaders, maintenance personnel, and quality assurance people.

2. Start as soon as the document becomes available.

3. Be sure people can easily access the documents they need.

4. Documents describe the one best way to run the process. Run the process accordingly.

5. For intermittent operation, refresher training is needed before each start.

CHAPTER 4

PROCESS DISCIPLINE FUNDAMENTALS: AUDITS

To do auditing well is to have mastered the true nature of process discipline, for it is in the feedback loops created by audits that you provide for the ongoing health of the entire system. The intent in establishing an audit program is to ensure that communication regarding the effectiveness of your efforts to run the process under process discipline takes place, and that it relays information about both your successes and your missteps. You can then reinforce what you are doing well and take corrective action where you discover inadequacies.

A successful audit program will include litmus tests for disclosing whether — and how well — you are meeting four objectives:

1. The operation is being run consistently, as it is documented.

2. Training of those who operate the process has been successful so that they know how to do their job correctly, including how to trouble-shoot problems they may experience during the course of their work.

3. The methods you have established for ensuring that non-standard situations are quickly resolved and the process is returned to standard are working well. Management

responds to the signals of system failure in ways that reinforce their dedication to process discipline.

4. Those who operate the process have easy access to clear, complete, correct, and current instructions for doing their job consistently.

The Audit System

Each organization can, and ought to, thoughtfully establish the frequency with which they will conduct their audits. Our experience has led us to recommend a two-tiered system: frequent and periodic. The frequent first-tier audits are conducted with regularity sufficient to the nature of the operations. Most plants refer to first-tier audits as "daily audits" (see Figure 4.1), but you must take into account that your particular operations might be intermittent in nature, or occur across three shifts on a seven-day schedule, or otherwise be more or less than "daily" in nature. The criterion for frequency, then, is "at a rate sufficiently often to quickly identify discrepancies before they cause quality or yield deterioration, become common practice, or embed themselves in our processes."

Second-tier audits are health-maintenance checks and are triggered either by elapsed time or by results of the first-tier audits. This makes sense, of course, if you extend the health-maintenance analogy and prescribe at least an annual physical (for the process discipline environment) in the absence of any other symptoms of disease or injury (say, for example, results from first-tier audits indicating systematic failure in the training plan for operators). Further, in light of what you may know about your genetic predisposition toward certain illnesses or occupational hazards inherent in your chosen profession, you might elect a more frequent checkup schedule in order to take corrective measures should problems be detected. If you know certain of your processes are more susceptible to process drift and have much higher personnel turnover than other areas, you might elect to audit these areas on a more frequent basis.

Figure 4.1 Daily Audit Example

Jamestown Plant DAILY AUDIT — VACUUM PLATING DEPARTMENT										
Instructions: Record all entries in ink. Circle discrepancies. Make one copy for Dept Supervisor.										
CRITICAL VARIABLE	Required Setting	Sat	Sun	Mon	Tue	Wed	Thu	Fri	Discrepancies MTD	YTD
1. DOCUMENTATION										
a. Serial Number must agree tag number.	Y									
b. SOP in use?	Y									
c. All ET's current?	Y									
2. Vacuum level (in microns)	≤ 550									
Check items 3 & 4 ONLY when operation is in Set-Up Mode during time of audit.										
3. Bellows vacuum valve open?	Y									
4. Rubber spacers attached to diaphragm valve?	2 spacers in place									
5. LOG BOOK ENTRY										
a. Serial # recorded?	Y									
b. Time entered (Hrs/Mins since capoff).	≥ 1 hr (60 min)									
c. Time On/Time Off (circ pump)	> 2 hrs									
6. Thermostat Setting (°C)	100-170									
7. Bell Jar Vacuum Valve (Open/Closed)	Closed									
8. Station Vacuum (Open/Closed)	Open									
9. Diaphragm (Open/Closed)	Open									
10. Black Cord Attached	Y									
11. Safety Gear Worn?	Y									
COMMENTS:										

Audit Series 003, Form # 5842333
Last Revised: 10/30/xx - Rev 042   Auditor: _____   Audit for Week Ending: _____

When results of first-tier audits indicate some fundamental breach of the discipline you are trying to instill, you must then initiate second-tier auditing to reinforce your commitment and to repair the damage that might otherwise continue to erode what gains you have made. Again, the health analogy should help you determine an appropriate course of action.

Who Should Perform the Audits

Deciding who will conduct the audits sometimes leads you down a slippery slope of compromise. While the notion of local control (that is, reducing hierarchy by pushing decision-making, authorization, and control downward to smaller and smaller subsets of the larger organization) is sound in theory, its application with regard to audits can lead to a fox-in-the-henhouse argument which undermines credibility of the results. No single answer can serve the wide variety of situations represented by our readers, but we can propose some guidelines that should suffice in a majority of operations:

- Those selected for conducting audits ought to have spotless reputations for integrity, independence, and fairness, so that energy is not wasted in disputing the accuracy of the results.

- Process knowledge is an asset, as is some familiarity with the department's equipment, but individuals who possess the attributes of integrity and fairness usually can be trained in the process details.

- Auditors must undergo the same training afforded to process operators in learning how to read gauges, take measurements and otherwise gather the output data to complete their records. Of course this training will include familiarization with the documents as well, since these serve as source material for constructing the audits in the first place.

- From time to time, on a random basis, knowledgeable and independent auditors from outside the direct local hierarchy should conduct the audits. We have found that this practice helps to prevent the pressure (from co-workers, department managers, "buddies", etc.) to report results which are favorably biased.

We have worked with factories that assigned audit duties in rotation across all personnel (including the plant manager) and departments. We have worked with factories that had as many as five or six full-time auditors. The distinguishing characteristics between those who were successful in using audits and those who were not lies not in how they organized the work, but rather in what they did with the results of the audits that were performed.

Selecting the Content of the Audit

As mentioned above, the documents that relate how the process operation is to be carried out serve as the source material for audit content. Likely candidates for inclusion in first-tier audits include:

- standard settings,
- key techniques,
- materials and tools in use,
- safety practices,
- equipment calibration, and
- actual readings from process instruments.

Collectively and collaboratively, the engineers, operators and production managers in a given area can review the process documentation to construct the initial audit in an area. This same group can establish the allowable ranges and tolerances for nominal settings. Periodic reviews of audit results will stimulate evolutionary refinement of content and adjustment of the frequency required to ensure consistent day-to-day operations.

The most efficient way to establish first-tier audits in a given area is to set up a meeting with those most knowledgeable about the process and ask the question: "What settings, tools, techniques, etc. are so important to the success of the operation that if they are done incorrectly we risk producing bad ware?" Add to the resulting list all of those practices you have inculcated in your operators as important to decreasing the amount of variability in the process. If the combined list is more than 50 items long, it is a good idea to assign each item an arbitrary (but unique) number and randomize the items such that a manageable number of them are checked each time the audit is conducted. Results can be entered into a spreadsheet program and tabulated over time. If certain items exhibit marked stability (in other words, no discrepancies are ever recorded) then perhaps they can be considered for periodic audit at some lower frequency.

The items you elect to include in process audits as an integral element of process discipline are not necessarily coincident with those items which deliver process control to the manufacturing operation, although there will be substantial overlap. In *process* audits you are monitoring your adherence to process discipline (including whether or not people have been trained to operate to standard, and whether everyone knows about impending process changes), rather than your ability to manufacture acceptable product.

For example, you audit whether or not the materials in use have shelf life expiration dates that have elapsed. Now it is certainly possible to make acceptable product using out-of-date materials, although in doing so you violate a basic tenet of process discipline. Despite the fact that the product meets all outgoing quality requirements, you nonetheless report this as a discrepancy since what you are auditing is your adherence to those practices which you know to yield the best results and the fewest problems over a sustained period.

The confusion and frustration which arises (chiefly among auditors and operators) as a result of management's failure to understand the difference between running the *process* the best way you know how and making *product* which meets your outgoing quality requirements has killed many audit programs. Bear in mind throughout all discussions of process audits that they are not intended as a substitute for process control. They represent a snapshot of the process, and their results are to be used to answer the question, "Are we running our processes the best way we know how?"

When to Conduct Audits

Since time-to-time, machine-to-machine, and operator-to-operator variability often are root cause sources of process problems, we strongly recommend audit coverage such that *if* there is variability present it will be swiftly detected. This recommendation should be extended to include off-shift operations where they exist, and sufficient randomness about the time that audits are conducted so that you disallow a situation where some operators or machines are always audited and others are never audited.

Within an organization there is often contention regarding whether it is better to conduct unannounced audits or to permit sufficient preparation prior to an audit so that the natural anxiety created by audit surveillance is reduced. Audits arouse in certain managers such territoriality that it is risky to encroach without prior permission. Nevertheless, we advocate randomness in the time, content, and personnel who conduct audits; and we do so simply because our experience tells us that this randomness affords more reliable data than other methods. We are, however, in favor of reporting to an area's team leader or manager that you are going to conduct an audit and inviting that person to accompany you as the audit is being conducted.

Audit Feedback and Reporting

At the conclusion of an audit, the people responsible for the area audited should receive immediate feedback on the results. Further, they ought to have the opportunity to discuss the results with the auditor, making appropriate comments for the record. A copy of the report should be left with the area management, although oral commentary can be substituted where audits have a strong and positive standing in the department.

Subsequent to completion of the audits, formal reports are issued from the compiled data. Each discrepancy is reported, usually accompanied by historic information (such as week-to-date and year-to-date summaries) about the repeat frequency so that trends can be spotted, and chronic problems can be addressed and resolved. Discrepancy resolution (corrective action) is assigned to a specific person or area of responsibility, with a due date for bringing the process back to best-known running conditions.

When audits are inaugurated, it is not uncommon for some people to complain that "policemen" have descended on the plant. Audit reports are resented; operators grumble about getting "gigged" on their audit. Having auditors "looking over our shoulders" is viewed as antithetical to an empowered workforce.

These reasons, and many others like them, are why we recommend that you pay careful attention to creating an environment where audits are regarded as helpful and productive. We have seldom run across operators who are not running the process to standard because they are trying to undermine the plant's ability to make acceptable product. Rather, plant management often puts its operators in a bind: run the operation to standard, and make acceptable product faster. Often these instructions are mutually exclusive, and your operators understand that they cannot win. They can run to standard, but not at acceptable rates. They can run fast, but the yields go down. They can make good product, but they have to move setpoints off standard. Well-conceived audits uncover these conflicts and permit you to make rational decisions that (over time) bring about optimized processes. In the absence of an active, effective audit program your operators make the trade-offs they feel most comfortable making — and that becomes a source of variability in the process through no fault of the operators involved.

The goodness of audits derives from the validity of their results and swift corrective action for reported discrepancies, and here lies your challenge. By design, audits expose the soft spots and weaknesses of the system you have constructed in order to deliver process discipline. Far too often organizations fail to resist the temptation to shoot the messenger, and thus undermine the very agency they have assigned to assist them in their improvement efforts. This dichotomy is not easily overcome, but it is in the response to audit results where successful organizations exhibit positive leadership in assigning corrective action swiftly and appropriately and without blame.

Each audit report must be treated as evidence that there are *specific actions* you can take to return the process to conditions you previously have determined to yield optimum results. The actions you take to swiftly resolve audit discrepancies signal to the factory the degree to which you seriously embrace the concepts of process discipline.

Getting It Done

1. Set up first-tier audits on a frequent basis — daily, once a shift, or less frequently for intermittent or job shop operations.

2. Set up second-tier audits, focusing on the process discipline system, on at least an annual basis. For troublesome or nascent operations, second-tier audits should be performed more frequently.

3. Develop audit content from the documents. Include settings, techniques, condition of materials and tools, safety practices, calibration, and output readings from process instruments.

4. Establish ranges and tolerances for the variables you plan to audit. These ranges and tolerances must be able to be met when the operation is being run as well as you know how to run it.

5. Report on the results within hours of conducting the audits. Note discrepancies, and be sure to record who is responsible for corrective action. Track results of corrective action.

6. Train people in the difference between *process* audits and *product* audits. Never stop communicating about what this difference implies.

7. Select auditors for integrity, independence, and process knowledge. Train them in the special requirements of auditing (including appropriate responses to pressures to bias audit results).

8. Establish independent audits.

9. Emphasize effective corrective action. Track and report audit results and trends, and correlate that data with corrective action.

CHAPTER 5

PROCESS DISCIPLINE FUNDAMENTALS: CONTROL OF CHANGE

Change control is the bedrock on which process discipline is founded. Few processes are robust enough to withstand the effects of shoddy implementation of change. If you examine your own processes and discover that the changes being made are chiefly "fixes" to process problems randomly encountered rather than controlled implementation of positive results from well-designed experiments, then it is time to evaluate the way that changes are made.

Certainly there are conditions under which you must make a change to respond to an unexpected problem or one that you have heretofore never encountered. Good change control systems will accommodate such circumstances by providing an emergency change process. All that is required is that the person who is responsible for introducing the change do what is necessary, then document it and submit it for review as soon as reasonable. When that review takes place, you can decide whether to submit a permanent change or to return the process to its prior status. In either event, you have added to your store of information about the things that can occur in the process and can upgrade your troubleshooting documentation to reflect this new experience.

Documentation of emergency changes proves to be a wonderful method for ensuring that the best of what you know and learn about the process is widely shared among those who need to know.

Likewise, from time to time you encounter the need to make a temporary fix to carry you over until a permanent solution is available. Some situations which come to mind are when equipment malfunctions or breaks down and you must find a workaround until it can be restored to service. Again, it is not difficult to accommodate such circumstances within a well-formulated system. The focus is on capturing the problem, determining the best approach for consistently responding to it, and reducing it to standard trouble-shooting practice.

The rate of change in manufacturing differs from operation to operation. Some processes may continue for weeks or even months with few changes required to take advantage of new technology or to resolve new problems or to meet new customer demands. Other processes may be so dynamic that whole departments must be created just to handle, record, copy, distribute revisions, and notify others of the changes taking place. Most of us work in environments that are somewhere in the middle; that is, a certain number of changes are incorporated into our processes every week.

It is important to distinguish when you are *controlling* the introduction of change and when you are merely *recording* change, providing mechanisms so that documents are updated and interested parties are aware that change has taken place. This chapter assumes that you have a documentation system that accurately describes the processes you manage today. It concentrates on those changes that you deliberately choose to make.

When Should Changes Be Considered?

Under what conditions should you allow changes to be made in the processes for which you are responsible? When you ask this question of groups of engineers, manufacturing managers and supervisors, technicians and operators and record their responses, you get a consistent list:

- there should be some proof that the change will work (i.e., data from valid experiment results),

- the process experts should be consulted and their approval obtained,

- you should be confident that no adverse consequences upstream or downstream will be incurred,

- the resulting process should be lower in cost, or at least no higher in cost (and this assumes a sophisticated and long-term view of the *overall* costs involved),

- interested parties should have a chance, *before* the change is made, to look it over and give advice,

- the change should represent a known improvement to the process,

- there should be training for those affected by the change.

Yet the same people who assembled the list above acknowledge that these conditions seldom prevail in their own factories. When we discuss the reasons why they fail to heed their own advice, they tell us that there is (perceived) pressure to respond to problems with an immediate "fix." This causes them, they say, to institute change without the control they believe is important. This constitutes an important *failure* in the regimen of process discipline, but it is a failure of management to create the required environment.

Change Control System Elements

So, then, what are the elements of a good change control system?

- You need a consistent way to gather information about proposed changes.

- You need to know what change you want to make and why you want to make it.

- You need proof that the change will produce the desired result.

- You need a timetable or chronological frame of reference so that you can distinguish product made *before* the change from product made *after* the change.

- You need some way to communicate with those who will be affected by the change.

The Form

We have included a single-sheet simplistic example of a form that contains the basic information required (see Figure 5.1). If it works for you, then use it. If you already have some form in use, check to ensure that it meets all the requirements we have outlined and, if it is lacking, modify it to include them. Once you have decided on the form you will use, set it up as a shareable template on whatever word processing package that you are using so that anyone can access the file and create a change proposal.

Describing the Change

There are many ways to describe the change so that it is clear what will happen when it takes place. In a macro sense, there are only three types of changes: additions, deletions, and changes to already documented information. If documents, drawings, or other entities are being changed, printing a copy of the source document and redlining the change is probably the most efficient way to show it. Likewise, you can indicate insertion points for new information and attach the necessary sheets. Occasionally you have to start from scratch with a whole new document. Just ensure that someone who is reviewing the change from the prospect of a year into the future will be able to tell with confidence what has changed. Nowadays, there are sophisticated software packages that enable you to scan in or import graphics and drawings and redline them electronically, although not every operation has access to these tools.

Figure 5.1 Process Documentation Change Control Form

PROCESS DOCUMENTATION CHANGE	DOCUMENT AFFECTED:	Tracking # _____

<table>
<tr><td>PROCESS DOCUMENTATION CHANGE
COPIES TO:
_____
_____
_____
_____</td><td>DOCUMENT AFFECTED:

Number   Title

☐ PERMANENT
☐ TEMPORARY
☐ EMERGENCY</td><td>Tracking # _____

EFFECTIVE: Date _____ Time _____
EXPIRATION: Date _____ Time _____</td></tr>
</table>

CHANGE FROM:	CHANGE TO:

REASON THIS CHANGE IS NECESSARY:
Attach Supporting Data

APPROVALS:

ORIGINATOR DATE	PROCESS ENGINEERING DEPT HEAD DATE PRODUCTION DEPT HEAD DATE
Tel. Contact: _____	
Pager #: _____	QUALITY ASSURANCE DATE OTHER DATE

Why You Are Making the Change

Sometimes you are making the change because the customer has made a specific request that you do so. (Bear in mind that the "customer" may be the next downstream operation rather than the external customer who buys your finished goods.) Sometimes you are responding to some regulatory change or external requirements; say, for example, when a raw material becomes unavailable or environmental concerns dictate you no longer use a certain chemical as your cleaning agent. Sometimes you are making the change because the new equipment you have purchased will enable you to increase the number of parts you pick up in a single pass or reduce the dwell time in the oven. It is important that you give the reason.

Some plants establish categories of reasons for tracking and reporting purposes, and this is worth considering in your own setup of change control. For example, it might be useful for trend analysis to know that 35% of your process changes during the last six months were originated as a result of direct requests from your customers. You decide the details of your system, so long as the basic elements are covered.

Proof

What is called for here is some cross-reference to the experiment that verified that the change would have the effect you desire and that there would be no unexpected adverse consequences insofar as you can reasonably tell. No change that omits this important element ought to be introduced into the process.

Of course there are sometimes valid proofs which do not entail a planned experiment. Process data, for example, can yield sufficient substantiation to convince you of the wisdom of the change. Our urging is that you scrupulously examine what the change originator offers to convince you that you ought to make the change in question. Where there are patterns of problems resulting from hastily introduced change, you can almost always trace back to a lack of rigor at this stage of change control.

Timing

Sometimes it is simple to say, "next Tuesday at 11:30 A.M. we will institute this change." Sometimes it is much more complex. There are two important pieces of information with regard to timing: 1) when are you *willing* to make the change and 2) when are you *ready* to make the change. For simple changes, the two points in time are coincidental; but some operations require that old stock be used before you change to new stock, or you must wait for the next job change, or the process change pertains only to a single product line and it is not yet scheduled for manufacture. If you remember that it is important to distinguish product made *before* the change is introduced from product made *after* the change is introduced, then it will be clear how you ought to track the timing information for your records. When you cannot know in advance of the specific time when the change will be introduced, you can specify the event that acts as the trigger for switching from old to new.

Communication

No other issue is so frequently cited as a source of error in implementing change. We have never heard manufacturing people complain that too much communication is taking place. The rule of thumb is that you can never be too thin or too rich or have too much communication. Do not overlook any of the following possibilities in your communication repertoire:

- Post the change at the workstation; have each operator initial it to indicate he or she has read it.
- Set up and use an e-mail "change alert" to all department managers.
- Use department bulletin boards to post changes.
- Publish weekly summaries of the changes taking place in the process.
- Discuss changes as a routine part of each morning production meeting.
- Discuss changes during crossover meetings at shift change.
- Keep a "change logbook" at the workstation, and record changes in it.

The More Things Change...

There are surely among the people in your organization those who strongly believe that engineers (and even certain operators) are capable enough, broad enough in their experience, and knowledgeable enough about the process that you ought to be willing to entrust them to make enlightened decisions about what changes are necessary. We have heard the dubious argument that an empowered workforce needs the ability to initiate changes as it sees fit without the folderol of formal change control.

If you are serious about process discipline, you must take special pains to address these arguments. *No* engineer, operator, or other person has the right to jeopardize your ability to make product by compromising the standard process through the introduction of uncontrolled change! It is as simple as that.

Getting It Done

1. Tailor our sample Process Document Change (PDC) form to your plant, or devise one of your own.

2. Teach the people in your plant — management, operating people, and support personnel — how the change control system will work. Change proposals must be submitted in advance and they must be supported by experimental data (or carefully measured process data) that prove that the change accomplishes its goal and has no adverse consequences. There must be an implementation plan that answers *when, where, whom, what products,* and *what equipment*. There must also be provision for training all involved personnel.

3. Familiarize the same groups with the emergency and temporary change procedures and when they are to be used.

4. Keep good records.

5. Remind all employees (and remind them frequently) about the crucial role of change control in maintaining process discipline.

CHAPTER 6

PROCESS DISCIPLINE FUNDAMENTALS: EXPERIMENTING ON THE MANUFACTURING PROCESS

There are three general ways to improve a manufacturing process: to run with ever-increasing consistency, to make individual changes to improve the process, and to identify fundamental new and better ways to run the process. The second two depend heavily on experimentation.

- The basic technique to justify a change to the process which a) assures that the change accomplishes its improvement objective, and b) protects against unforeseen adverse consequences, is to run a confirming experiment before implementing the change.

- The fundamental way to improve the process is to explore some other region(s) of operation experimentally (sometimes these other regions are provided by different equipment). Try to determine if any domain provides better overall results than your current operating points. If a region of better operation *is* identified, you should probably run *another* experiment to confirm the result. Usually, you would also explore that region more intensely to be sure you have found the *optimal* new place to be operating. The experimental exploration may be by computer simulation, but you would still want to confirm experimentally in all but the simplest cases.

Experimentation is the most important and the most difficult of the systems to achieve process improvement. However, a good program of process experimentation directly impacts the rate of process improvement, and provides the most likely route to competitive advantage. It is hard, most people do not do it well, and if you learn to do it with consistent excellence, you will assuredly progress against the competition, and will frequently gain a forefront position.

It takes a variety of skills and knowledge to do process experimenting well, and none of the books the authors know—some of which are classics in a specific field—come close to addressing the range of issues which should be covered. Here are some of the issues:

1. the strategy of experimentation;

2. the statistics of experimentation, especially statistically designed experiments;

3. how to plan an experiment that will run flawlessly in an operating factory, avoiding known pitfalls;

4. communicating, selling, gaining approval and support, and resources for the experiment;

5. recording the results so they become part of the plant/technology's permanent storehouse of process knowledge and are readily accessible;

6. taking appropriate action on the experimental results.

There are numerous important sub-issues, but they can fit under one of these umbrellas. We will summarize some experts' ideas on item one, the strategy. We address statistics of experimentation briefly and generally, because many excellent books are available on this subject, and professional statisticians are well versed in the material. We focus our attention on items three through six, which are not cerebral enough for much scholarly literature and which often determine whether the whole thing works anyway (and which we know something about).

Experiment Basics

Let us define an "experiment" as "a temporary trial of a different-than-standard process to generate data that support a new process or justify a process change."

The first thing to know about the strategy of experimentation is that it is highly beneficial to have a statistician participating in the design and planning of an experiment if at all possible. The second choice, if involvement of a statistician is not feasible, is to use an engineer or scientist who has training and experience in the use of statistics in experimentation. However, an organization that is committed to process improvement for quality improvement, cost reduction, and increased throughput (to developing a process discipline environment) can benefit greatly by employment of a competent statistician — far more than the cost of the additional individual.

You first need to dispel the old myth about experimentation that it is desirable to run "change one variable at a time" experiments. Quite the opposite! When you change only one variable at a time, you lose in two ways:

The most important way you lose is that you will *never* be able to identify any interactions between variables. What this means is that "one variable at a time" experimentation presupposes that all variables are unaffected by the level of the other variables in the system. So, if you check the output of the system while you change only variable A over some range, you are assuming that the impact of A's change on the system is unaffected by the levels of variables B, C, D, E, etc. Very often this is not true. It is particularly not true in familiar manufacturing situations, such as combined time and temperature variation in chemical or thermal processes. For this reason, one variable at a time experiments will give an incorrect result.

Further, any interactions between or among variables can never be discovered. Since interactions are common and quite important in manufacturing, this severely constrains your ability to learn about the process.

Another significant weakness in the one-at-a-time approach is that it turns out to be less efficient — it takes more experimentation (and time and money) to acquire the same amount of data.

Experimenting in an Operating Factory

When you design and plan an experiment to run in a factory, you should have at least three major objectives:

1. to assure that the experiment will be conducted with consideration of statistical significance, paired controls through the standard process, randomization, calibration of measuring instruments, and oversight to control the identity and flow of the parts;

2. to get the most valid data from the scarce and costly production time and resources which have been allocated;

3. to assure that you are aware of all experiments in progress and their effects and results, so they are not allowed to interfere (or conflict) with each other, and that any process difficulties which result from an experiment are clearly traceable to their source.

Here are some items that need to be reviewed in order to achieve the objectives listed:

1. Is the sample size sufficient for statistical significance? What must the difference be between the alternatives to prove the hypothesis, and at what confidence level will it be demonstrated? How variable is the present process for

the parameter(s) being tested, and what does that imply about sample size, number of replicates, and test duration to assure convincing results?

2. Statistically designed multivariable experiments should be used wherever possible because they can uncover interactions and require less testing to get the same amount of data. They should not be attempted without availability of a trained person, however.

3. Measuring instruments used in the experiment should be calibrated immediately prior to the experiment where appropriate, and may need to be recalibrated before the experiment is completed.

4. Randomizing and blocking should be used to prevent confounding of the experimental results. For instance, if you are testing furnace No. 1 against furnace No. 2, the parts being processed through furnace No. 1 should not be from supplier Jones made on the night shift by Tom while the parts processed through furnace No. 2 come from supplier Smith made on the day shift by Mary. The suppliers, the operators, and the shifts should be deliberately randomized so you can be sure that the experimental results are not "confounded" by differences in those other factors. Randomizing is not an offhand activity. It is usually done by statistically qualified persons using tables of random numbers.

5. When running an experiment in the factory, it is usually necessary to provide "coverage" on the floor by an individual who thoroughly understands the details of the experiment, and assures that it is being processed correctly.

6. Most experiments, to be useful, are set up as a comparison between two or more alternatives, one of those being the present standard (often called "controls"). You need to be sure that the present standard group is supervised and run just as carefully as you run the new hopefuls group.

It is also desirable to set aside a small number of the parts selected for test processing, and hold them out in case the experiment results raise some question about the characteristics of the parts that were tested. In some cases, the initial plan could benefit if some units were held out at other process steps.

7. All experiments should be documented in a survivable way, irrespective of the results. Every plant should establish minimum standards for what is required in the report. To assure future cooperation, the report should be disseminated to everyone who participated in the experiment. It is even better to hold a meeting to review the results and recommended action with those same people shortly after issuing the report. Experiment reports should be maintained permanently in an accessible, orderly file.

    Some plants report only those experiments that have positive results. Negative (and therefore unexpected) results need to be reported as well so that the experiment is not replicated later.

8. A carefully written experiment plan is the most important determinant of success of experiments run in the factory.

9. On complex experiments, it is beneficial to hold a brief shakedown run using the same measuring instruments, data sheets, and people doing the things planned for the experiment. A short meeting afterward can usually solicit ideas that improve and simplify the procedure.

10. It is almost always better to run several smaller experiments than one large one. The practical difficulty of keeping control of the experiment rises exponentially with the number of variables and with the number of levels being evaluated.

11. It is critical to concentrate on running the experiment exactly as planned, *and not to try to change or adjust anything so as to make good, saleable product.* All participants must

understand this from the start to preclude well-intentioned actions that would ruin the experimental results.

We often start the discussion on this subject in a course we give with the question, "How many of you have run an experiment in a plant and lost some of the parts, or had them intermixed with standard production ware, or had them scrapped because they looked or measured different from standard product, or had them packed and shipped to the customer before they were ever evaluated?" We instructors always raise our hands, as do the experienced and truthful participants. Many things can go wrong, and they often do, but the good news is that almost all the pitfalls are preventable, and it only takes good thorough planning to avoid them; it almost never requires deep technical knowledge or analysis.

Some of the best-known statistics books suggest that experimentation should be thought of as an iterative process. They describe it as a learning process, and indicate that the experimenter should expect to make some mistakes, and should learn enough from them to home in on his target after a few tries. This is a valid perspective for research in the laboratory, and often for development in the pilot facility. However, when you run an experiment in a factory, your objective should be to run one experiment (not one run) which will give you clear facts and distinctions so that you can make a decision on whether and how to change the process. In the factory, you are usually experimenting on a process that is established enough to run in production. You may be aware of the limitations of your knowledge, and of your inability to predict outcomes, but you are almost always starting from a better base in the plant. For instance, you should have a good idea of which are the important variables to include in the experiment, and where the extreme variable limits are beyond which the process is unlikely to function.

Furthermore, access to the process is much more expensive, and frequently more restricted, so it is important to make maximum use of the opportunities you get. If you need to run another experiment or a follow-on experiment, it is often because you did an inadequate job of planning your original experiment. Although there are some specific technical exceptions, it is best for you to plan an experiment for immediate implementation if results are positive; you should plan to prove conclusively that your hypothesis is valid, conclusively enough to implement with the facts (data) you have elicited from this experiment. This may seem obvious, but in the authors' experience, in practice it is the exception rather than the rule. Most often, additional follow-on experiments have to be run before you accumulate enough data to justify a process change. A retrospective analysis generally shows that the experiment could have been structured so as to avoid further iterations. The most common error is that the sample size is too small to provide enough confidence to justify the process change.

Careful experiment planning not only can avoid the need for a sequence of several experiments, it can also give you much of what you need to justify and sell the experiment. The plan helps you to identify the actions needed to run complex experiments flawlessly, and it prepares you to record the experiment results comprehensively and accurately. The plan also prepares the organization for the action that must be taken to implement important experimental results.

Perhaps even more vital, the plan is the basic communications tool that tells operators, supervisors, and management why the experiment is being run, what will happen and when (including any potential adverse consequences), and what their individual responsibilities will be. The experiment plan also details the specific construction of the experiment so it can be critiqued, and perhaps improved, by people other than its author.

Experiment Plan Requirements

The experiment plan is a formal document that should be prepared and approved prior to each experiment. It provides information about the objectives, benefits, costs, risks, and, particularly, detailed information about how the experiment is to be conducted. The latter includes sample sizes, which variables will be manipulated and to what levels, which variables will be held constant, what measuring instruments will be used and how frequently they will be calibrated, how and where and when the data will be recorded, and, most important, who is in charge. The plan should also describe how the process and equipment would be returned to standard operating conditions. (See Figures 6.1 and 6.2 for a sample blank experiment plan and checklist and a completed example.)

Figure 6.1 Experiment Plan & Experiment Checklist

EXPERIMENT PLAN	
EXPERIMENT PLAN	ORIGINATOR: _____ DEPARTMENT DATE
COPIES TO: _____ _____ _____ _____	EXPERIMENT COORDINATOR: _____
	Tel. Contact: _____ START: _____ DATE TIME
	Pager # : _____ FINISH: _____ DATE TIME

1. OBJECTIVES OF THIS EXPERIMENT

2. BENEFITS OF THIS EXPERIMENT
CONFIDENCE LEVEL: _____
POTENTIAL SAVINGS TO THE PLANT IN ONE CALENDAR YEAR: $_____

3. PROCESS PARAMETERS TO BE VARIED	4. PARAMETERS TO BE CONTROLLED/MONITORED

APPROVALS:		
	PROCESS ENGINEERING DEPT HEAD DATE	PRODUCTION DEPT HEAD DATE
STATISTICIAN DATE	QUALITY ASSURANCE DATE	EQUIP ENGINEERING DEPT HEAD DATE (If equipment modifications are part of this experiment)

Figure 6.1 Experiment Plan & Experiment Checklist (cont.)

EXPERIMENT PLAN

5. CRITERIA WHICH WILL BE USED TO EVALUATE RESULTS OF THIS EXPERIMENT

6. SET UP PROCEDURES FOR THIS EXPERIMENT (Attach additional sheets if necessary)

7. EXPOSURE COSTS / RISK ASSESSMENT	8. OUT OF POCKET EXPENSES

9. DATE REPORT DETAILING RESULTS OF THIS EXPERIMENT WILL BE SUBMITTED: _____   PERSON RESPONSIBLE FOR SUBMITTING RESULTS REPORT: _____

Normally, the experiment plan is written by the person who wants to conduct the experiment, but occasionally a more experienced individual will devise a plan for someone who has a good experimental idea, but may not be the right one to document it. The author of the plan usually is the person who must write an experiment report when the experiment is concluded.

Every experiment must be reported in detail, because that is a principal way for the organization to capture and keep process learning. Sometimes, people who run experiments that do not

Figure 6.1 Experiment Plan & Experiment Checklist (cont.)

EXPERIMENT PLAN CHECKLIST

EXPERIMENT OBJECTIVES
- ☐ Does this experiment build on prior experimental work?   Identify such work.
- ☐ Is the plan consistent with the objectives as stated?

BENEFITS OF THIS EXPERIMENT
- ☐ Are the results of this experiment going to be used to justify process change?
- ☐ Will the experiment prove or explain a theory not adequately understood before?
- ☐ Estimate the dollars which will be saved in 12 months if this experiment is successful.

PROCESS PARAMETERS TO BE VARIED
- ☐ Is there an experimental design matrix available?
- ☐ Will there be a "recovery" time for equipment and/or process to reach equilibrium between test runs?
- ☐ How will each parameter be varied? In what increments? Who will make the changes?

PROCESS PARAMETERS TO BE CONTROLLED/MONITORED
- ☐ Which parameters will be controlled? And which will be monitored?
- ☐ How frequently will measurements/observations be recorded? By whom?
- ☐ Which instruments must be calibrated before, during, after this experiment?

CRITERIA USED TO EVALUATE EXPERIMENT RESULTS
- ☐ Have we predetermined our success/failure criteria so as to avoid bias once experiment is complete?
- ☐ Which output variables will be measured?
- ☐ Can response variables be measured with sufficient accuracy and precision to meet objectives?
- ☐ What benchmark measurements will be used for comparison with experimental results?

SETUP PROCEDURES
- ☐ Are sufficient materials in place to conduct this experiment?
- ☐ Has provision been made to accurately identify, quarantine and store experimental product?
- ☐ Has adequate provision been made for coverage, tracking and supervision of the experiment?
- ☐ Are sample sizes adequate to achieve the experimental objectives?
- ☐ Have production operators received sufficient information to properly support this experiment?

EXPOSURE COSTS / RISK ASSESSMENT
- ☐ What is the worst that can happen if the experiment goes awry?
- ☐ Do we expect to incur machine/equipment downtime to transition back to pre-experimental conditions?

OUT OF POCKET EXPENSES
- ☐ What is the value of the product and materials used in this experiment?
- ☐ How will the experimental product be dispositioned? Sold to customers? Destroyed?

---

achieve their objective are slow or reluctant to write their report. Actually, it is more important to report these failures, because the result was unexpected, which means there is an opportunity for new learning. Most people are pleased to write comprehensive reports about successful experiments that promise financial benefits to the organization.

The experiment plan should usually be two or three pages long, depending on the complexity level of the experiments gen-

Figure 6.2 Experiment Plan (Filled-In Example)

| EXPERIMENT PLAN | ORIGINATOR: __Pascal Gauss__ ___ETCH___ __4 Apr__ |
| | DEPARTMENT   DATE |

COPIES TO: EXP #: __#4801__   EXPERIMENT COORDINATOR: _____ **Ben Franklin** _____

DaVinci ___

Galileo ___ E.Curie ___   Tel. Contact: __x1213__   START: __17 Apr__ __00:01__

Maxwell ___   DATE   TIME

Pasteur ___ ___   Pager # : __555-9998__   FINISH: __18 Apr__ __23:59__

___ ___   DATE   TIME

1. OBJECTIVES OF THIS EXPERIMENT

Determine if tensile strength of product -14 can be significantly improved with small changes in temperature and concentration of the acid in the etch bath. Can it be done without major cost increase or adverse quality or safety results?

2. BENEFITS OF THIS EXPERIMENT

Customers A and B have been pressing us for increased tensile strength (>15%). We can protect a large profitable business if we can supply stronger product.

CONFIDENCE LEVEL: __75%__

POTENTIAL SAVINGS TO THE PLANT IN ONE CALENDAR YEAR: $1.5 Million

3. PROCESS PARAMETERS TO BE VARIED

High, Low and Center Values of Concentration & Temperature as shown:

- Run High & Low concentration at all 3 temperatures.
- Run Center concentration only at 35°, but run 3 replicates.

	HIGH	CENTER	LOW
Concentration	28%	26%	24%
Temperature	38 °C	35 °C	32 °C

4. PARAMETERS TO BE CONTROLLED/MONITORED

- Product -14
- Standard Cycle Time
- Randomize Run Order

Start experiment with fresh acid solution. Add 100% acid or distilled water. Remove some etch solution as necessary.

Allow time for temperature to reach equilibrium.

Run process strictly to S.O.P.

APPROVALS:

| _Lavoisier_ 4/07 | _Wuensch_ 4/07 |
| PROCESS ENGINEERING DEPT HEAD DATE | PRODUCTION DEPT HEAD DATE |

Fisher 4/07

STATISTICIAN   DATE

Shewhart 4/08	_Whitney_ 4/08
QUALITY ASSURANCE DATE	EQUIP ENGINEERING DEPT HEAD DATE
	(If equipment modifications are part of this experiment)

erally run in the plant. Here are the important items that should be boxes on the form and should be filled out for each experiment:

1. experimenter's name, phone extension, e-mail address, location, title, department;

2. signature and date for experimenter; start date, completion date, report date;

Figure 6.2 Experiment Plan (Filled-In Example) (Cont.)

EXPERIMENT PLAN

5. CRITERIA WHICH WILL BE USED TO EVALUATE RESULTS OF THIS EXPERIMENT

Differences in mean and standard deviation of tensile test values. All samples will be tested until fracture.

6. SET UP PROCEDURES FOR THIS EXPERIMENT
    (Attach additional sheets if necessary)

At the end of the 16:00-24:00 shift, on April 16, empty and clean the acid tank in the etcher.
Fill with fresh acid corresponding to the first run.
Adjust temperature and arrive at equilibrium.
Run 50 parts of Product -14 units (complete up to the etch operation).
Adjust acid concentration for each subsequent run by adding 100% acid or water.
Remove solution volume equal to the amount added.
Pick 25 pieces randomly from each run and run tensile test.
Record data, calculate mean and standard deviation of each group.
Reserve the other 25 pieces from each group (in case questions arise later).
At the end of the experiment, establish standard acid bath setup for production startup.
During experiment, process parts strictly to standard operating procedure.

7. EXPOSURE COSTS / RISK ASSESSMENT	8. OUT OF POCKET EXPENSES
No significant exposure.	Cost of product used in this experiment. Cost of acid and disposal. Overtime labor to run experiment. Estimated total: $3,700

9. DATE REPORT DETAILING RESULTS OF THIS EXPERIMENT WILL BE SUBMITTED: ___April 22___

  PERSON RESPONSIBLE FOR SUBMITTING RESULTS REPORT: ___Pascal Gauss___

3. sign-off list with space for initials and date — minimum should include managers (or other senior representatives) of production, engineering, and quality control; and additional lines should be provided for more complex experiments (which require further approvals). Experiment plans should be routinely referred to, and approved by, any other persons who have special knowledge or experience in the

technology or operating area being tested, equipment or material being evaluated, etc. The plan's preparer should try to get the document reviewed by anyone who can contribute to the betterment of the experiment, or who can verify (or challenge) the need for the evaluation;

4. quantified benefits (the purpose of the experiment) should the experiment succeed;

5. cost of running the experiment, description of risk exposures, and potential costs if the risks are not avoided;

6. complete description of the experiment, including:

   - number of conditions,
   - number of runs,
   - number of samples per run,
   - schematic of experiment design,
   - how samples and sequences will be randomized,
   - how and when the process will be prepared for the experiment,
   - how and when the process will be returned to normal operation status, and
   - which equipment/lines will be used;

7. which parameters will be deliberately varied, how and when that will be done, and how long to allow to reach equilibrium conditions before or between test runs;

8. which parameters will be held constant and at what levels, and which ones will be allowed to float, and whether or when data will be recorded for these variables;

9. what measuring instruments must be calibrated, when/how often, how it should be done, which output variables should be measured, and how and where data should be recorded;

10. what criteria will be used to determine the action to be taken or the judgment of success or failure;

11. who is responsible for the overall management of the experiment and who is responsible for any particular phases.

This seems like a formidable list of detailed information to prepare — and it is. But this material is needed to run the experiment as intended, and this is exactly the kind of planning which prevents mistakes and allows you to perform a complicated procedure correctly the first time. The proposer of an experiment who is not ready to answer any of these questions may not be prepared to run the experiment in the plant.

Incidentally, it is important to copy or notify all those people who need to know some of this information to perform their experimental tasks properly or to be sure people, materials and tooling required are available and people have been briefed. You need to think about shift supervisors, team leaders, technicians, associates, operators, quality and maintenance personnel, and production planners and material handlers, as well as statisticians, engineers, and scientists.

Of course, whenever an experiment is run in a factory on production equipment, resource is being allocated to the experiment that is therefore unavailable to make product for customers. The person in charge of the experiment must work with production management to schedule the experiment for the most convenient window. It is crucial that when the window arrives, everything is available and ready, and all participants have been communicated with and trained as appropriate. Frequently, experiments for problem solving or process improvement are needed when recent production results have not been good, and access to the production line for experimentation is only grudgingly available. At such times, it is essential that the experiment be carried out on schedule and without error to avoid embarrassment and preclude the need for additional process time.

You need to run a variety of experiments in manufacturing. These might be characterized by some of the following questions that need to be answered:

a) Where is the best point in this domain to operate?

b) Does material A perform as well as or better than material B or not?

c) Have we eliminated problem P by changing R?

d) What are the important variables to control in this new process?

e) Which variables most strongly influence dimension A or performance feature B, in which direction, and how much?

f) Which combination of sequential treatments provides the best overall output or quality?

If you can develop models for these experiments and can learn to implement them, most of the experimentation needs in manufacturing will be covered. That is not to say that one model will satisfy the needs for each generic question listed; it will not, but even one model for each question will be a major enabler for experimenters in the plant.

It is beyond the scope of this book to provide illustrative examples for these questions, because the specific experiment structure depends on the nature of the process and on what information is known (or can be measured) and what is not known. The best alternative is to secure the assistance of a qualified statistician. We do provide a bibliography of some excellent reference books at the end of this chapter, but they will not make a neophyte into a competent practitioner.

People structuring experiments in the plant should make use of all the technical knowledge they have of the process. For instance, if they think that a certain output varies as the square of an input variable, the experiment's design should make use of that. You may sometimes be in error, and you will learn that, but most of the time the experiment will be improved by using as much process knowledge as you have.

When you are working with very limited experience and knowledge, as you might be on a new process that is still quite developmental, it is often wise to first run a "screening" experiment to identify which are the important variables having significant effects on the process. There are special statistical techniques for this. Fortunately, the statistics also tell you how much of the total process variability is explained by your choices. By examining the unexplained "residuals," you can usually determine if you missed any important ones, and you might have to try again with some additional variables in the screening experiment. When you are pretty sure that the important ones are all identified, you can proceed with your experimental program.

Excellent software packages are now available that take most of the work out of statistical design and analysis, and provide graphic outputs which help to communicate the important conclusions from the data. These should also be used by knowledgeable professionals.

Converting Experiments Into Better Manufacturing

The entire purpose of experimentation is to identify some action that can be taken to improve the process. Until you convert your experimental learning into action that improves the process, your purpose is unfulfilled. The experimenter must drive to get the action implemented. His goal is not improved information; it is a better working process. This is often a more difficult objective than you might think. Operating people are sometimes skeptical about the unfamiliar. They may question the robustness of the new operating conditions, or whether the same result will really occur next time. If the experimental program is conducted competently, the answers will be positive.

The experimenter should prepare the operating people well in advance for the *beneficial* consequences of the work. Operating managers should be prime movers in the discussions on what the appropriate action and implementation program should be. Then they will want to take maximum advantage of the new information.

Summarizing some actions the experimenter should take:

1. Discuss the potential benefits, costs, and risks with key production managers — jointly, if possible — to assure that they understand and concur in the logic of the experiment and the benefits claimed.

2. Be especially open to any suggested modifications that do not undermine the effectiveness of the experiment.

3. After a draft of the experiment plan is written, review it again. Again, solicit ideas for improvement. This is the time to seek *commitment to implementation* if and when the experiment yields the expected results.

4. The experiment's results may be somewhat different than expected, but still generally positive. Be prepared (if necessary) to repeat the experiment with or without changes, to revise the proposed action to change the process, or to delay implementation until better methodology is available, depending on the views of production management.

Annotated Bibliography for Experimentation

Box, George E.P., William G. Hunter, and J. Stuart Hunter. *Statistics for Experimenters.* **New York: John Wiley & Sons, 1978.** This is the bible. It is totally authoritative and reliable, and its authors were the world's best. It is realistic and somewhat practical. It suffers only from the fact that the writers were all professors. It has a lot of mathematics, and readers sometimes feel they must go back to school to really understand and make use of the book. The authors clearly made decisions in favor of rigor rather than comprehension and simplicity, although the book is described by them as a "first course."

Nevertheless, every self-respecting statistician and many engineers have it on their shelves, and refer to it first. Every plant with a process to improve should have a copy. We just wish they had published an easier version for the general reader.

Traver, Robert W. *Industrial Problem Solving.* **Carol Stream, IL: Hitchcock Publishing Co., 1989.** Many working engineers and a large number of statisticians have a copy of this very useful guide squirreled away. The book shows, in clear and reasonably comprehensible language, how to solve a fair number of "typical" and generally simple manufacturing problems with techniques that make use of basic statistical logic, but avoid classical statistical analysis. This book teaches "how to do" much more than it explains "why it works," and that is fine. It takes the risk of some occasional misapplication, but assumes successful usage most of the time.

We think the author has made a good bargain, but we would be happier if Traver stressed the benefits of an available statistician, with whose assistance the probability of success could be near 100%.

The book is organized as a collection of stories, with the solutions, assumed to have been worked out by the author, seeming to be very simple (and some are). So it provides a selection of arrows for the quiver, but not a logic tree for approaching general or complex problems.

It does not emphasize the building and implementation of either systems of problem prevention or of preservation of learning, but assumes that the job is very nearly over when the root cause analysis is completed. Of course, he shares this naive viewpoint with many other statistical authors. However, when one of Traver's techniques fits a practitioner's current problem situation, the joy of the process problem solver can be tremendous. This is a great little book, with something for almost everyone in the business.

Western Electric Company Inc. *Statistical Quality Control Handbook.* **Easton, PA: Mack Publishing Company, 1956.**
A terrific volume to which all manufacturing problem solvers should have ready access. It is the classic description of statistical process control, and for that alone it is worth its weight in gold. Let us hope that with the disappearance of the authoring company and its parent (in prior structure, if not current totality), a way will be found to keep this in print for another century.

As Mozart is reputed to have said as he listened to a piece by Bach, "one can learn something from this."

Fisher, Sir Ronald A. *The Design of Experiments,* **7th ed. New York: Hafner Publishing Co., 1971.**
First published in 1935, this is a jewel of a book by the brilliant man who formulated statistical problem solving as a science — and who created practically all of it. His clear and concise language as he explains the fine points makes one proud to be using this material. This is a volume for inspiration and for understanding the whys and distinctions. Fisher did most of his work in agricultural experimentation, so there is not much direct carryover to manufacturing, but he is understandable and crystal clear.

Box, George E.P., and Norman R. Draper. *Empirical Model Building and Response Surfaces.* **New York: John Wiley & Sons, 1987.**
People whose processes are understood well enough to make use of this volume usually already know about this book. It is another bible from George Box, the final word on the topics. For those of you progressing up the understanding and control ladder, and arriving at the point where you might make use of these more advanced techniques, this is the volume for guidance.

Lochner, Robert H., and Joseph E. Matar. *Designing for Quality.* **New York: Quality Resources, 1990.**
This book has an interesting modern point of view, and discusses how one integrates ideas such as *concurrent engineering* and *use of teams* with standard statistical efforts. It contains some good illustrative examples, and suggests some interesting graphical methods for simpler solutions.

The authors go down the Genichi Taguchi route pretty far, however, claiming "it's all the same in the end," and passing over the issues of impracticality of great numbers of replications, and of requirements for data from conditions of little interest. They do, however, sometimes offer more conventional analyses of the problems.

Here are a few suggestions for our readers in their choice of statistics books for guidance and self-help:

- If you cannot understand the chapter headings, it is probably not the book for you.

- If there is a lot of mathematics, and most of it makes your eyes glaze over, it is probably not the book for you.

- If there are a lot of *it is obvious thats* that are not obvious to you, *similarlys* that do not seem similar, and other skips and jumps which you have difficulty following, it is probably not the book for you.

Authors try to reach different audiences. Sometimes they want to be very rigorous, perhaps to impress academic peers. Sometimes they want to stress their originality and creativity by approaching traditional problems in nontraditional ways. Sometimes they want to make the subject as understandable and easy and useful as possible for the practitioner who reads the book. Try to find a volume by someone who seems to fit this last mold.

There are now available a number of statistical software packages of significant capability. The software market is so dynamic, however, that we are reluctant to recommend (or even comment on) the relative merits of various offerings, because something much more useful may emerge tomorrow.

The software vendors have eliminated most of the drudgery of statistical analysis and problem solving, and provide graphic outputs of substantial power and flexibility. The packages generally lead the user through the setup and design of the experiment, and, later, the analysis and presentation of the data. The major challenge is being sure that the correct methods and alternatives are selected for the particular situation.

Experimenters should familiarize themselves with several of the packages, and make use of the one that seems to be most suitable.

CHAPTER 7

THE ROLE OF COMPUTERS AND INFORMATION TECHNOLOGY

The Value of Computerization

Decades ago when we first formulated process discipline as a strategic system for manufacturing management, our implementation tools consisted of IBM Selectric® typewriters, cut-and-paste techniques for illustrating documents, calculators to sum and average audit totals, hand-lettered overhead transparencies, and bulky file cabinets to keep everything in order. Those tasked with producing documents, conducting audits, training, and administration chronically complained that there was too much to do and too little time to do it all. Updating the documents, distributing change control information and experiment plans, and ensuring that overhead transparencies used in training were current and correct required teams of people to type and copy and file and correct and issue and post at workstations.

Word processing makes editing and updating process documents simple and fast. Document distribution is accomplished through electronic networking and file cabinets are disappearing. Audit programs use simple spreadsheets to tally data, perform analyses, and generate meaningful statistics to guide decision-making. Experiment plans can be constructed by using interactive programs that pilot the originator through a series of questions and checklists and then eject a customized plan that exactly fits the requirements.

Not only do computers eliminate much of the tedium and redundancy inherent in paper-based systems, but they also give rise to opportunities early practitioners of process discipline could not have imagined. Here are a few examples:

- Documents, change control forms, and experiment plans which require approval before implementation can now be processed in parallel, thus significantly reducing cycle time.

- Approval signatures can be gathered and editorial annotations can be added in whatever sequence that is deemed desirable, then fed back to the originator electronically.

- Forms for initiating change control, experiments, audits, or other more peripheral tasks can be committed to templates callable from any workstation in the factory.

- Feedback loops can be created such that operators on the shop floor can highlight difficult or incorrect passages in documents, then signal for improved clarity or additional information by attaching these to e-mail messages sent to a central coordinator for disposition.

- Auditors can use simple spreadsheets to sort audit data so that patterns can be identified and graphic presentations of results can highlight areas requiring corrective action.

- Cross-referencing related documents can be accomplished through use of hypertext markup links (html) which use point-and-click technology to navigate through multiple source documents.

- Training sessions designed using interactive programs are not only more interesting but also more effective. They have the advantage of creating a feedback loop to ensure that trainees understand how to use the information.

Migrating From Paper Systems

Occasionally we encounter early adopters of process discipline who are still using paper as their primary medium for shop floor information. Heavily invested in the methods they have developed which have served them well in the past, they are often reluctant to engage in the new technologies that promise rejuvenation of their obsolete systems. Reshaping the way they manage the administrative aspects of process discipline can be threatening to those who are vested in the status quo.

If your organization is struggling with migration from paper systems, it may be necessary to structure a special project to undertake the required initiatives. A simple test of whether or not you fit this category is to ask yourself if longer than six months has elapsed between the decision to convert and significant progress in making the actual transition. If no concrete plan has emerged within that time frame, it is likely that the information and/or skills you need have not yet been identified.

Conversion to electronic media is a requirement for staying even in the marketplace, and those who do it best will gain competitive advantage. Most factories now invest as heavily in computers and peripherals as they do for traditional capital equipment used to manufacture product. If you are struggling with migrating from paper systems, you will need to partner with the appropriate information systems resources (either internal or external to your own organization) in order to make a successful transition.

Fortunately, the tools required to make these transitions are cheap and powerful. Personal computer users exchanging disks and using the Internet for e-mail can be as effective for small organizations as massive mainframes using distributed networks are for large ones. There is no longer an economic barrier to deter the application of technology to the tasks at hand.

Since computer tools are evolving so rapidly, and since we ourselves are not experts in the information systems field, here we will concentrate on accessing and identifying the tools you need rather than describing them in detail. We strongly recommend that you seek advice on which software and hardware are appropriate for your needs from competent professionals, looking first within your own organization and turning for external help only if your internal resources are inadequate for the task.

- Any of the major word-processing programs offered with office suite software provide opportunities to create document templates which speed the document-creation task and ensure consistency. In addition, merge-text features permit boilerplate text to feed into multiple documents.

- Investing in a scanner provides the ability to improve the quality of illustrations associated with documentation. It also affords the opportunity to incorporate signature facsimiles as approval authorization.

- Point-and-click macros that simplify repetitive tasks can be created even by those with no programming background.

- Any of the spreadsheet applications easily incorporates graphics for charting audit results. These programs can also track document writing progress for new process discipline efforts.

- Change control logs can be created in either spreadsheets or word processing.

- E-mail generates a myriad of opportunities for communicating about every aspect of your process discipline program.

These are only a few of the possibilities for launching electronic enhancements either in tandem with or as replacements for paper systems.

System Conversions

Making the decision to move from paper-based to electronic systems is in many ways easier than deciding to convert from one electronic system to another. Operations sometimes outgrow their initial applications but become stymied by the enormity of the task of migration to newer, better-suited software.

Concurrent with implementation of any of the elements associated with process discipline, you will want to consider whether or not system conversion ought to be part of the program. In most cases, you can benefit by incorporating the conversion along with the rest of the process discipline initiatives. An umbrella project will require close coordination with your information systems resources so that the entire project is well integrated.

Perhaps the most common problem which arises once the decision has been made to undergo a conversion from one system to another is associated with the structure of the time element of the project. Given a choice between a timely but resource-intensive conversion and an extended schedule with no apparent additional resource burden, some plants opt for an elongated schedule under which two systems must be simultaneously maintained under two separate sets of requirements. Be careful here, though. Unless special provision has been made to resource sufficiently to account for the dual maintenance, one or the other system suffers from inadequate attention and consequences are often severe. Once the downslide begins, it is even more difficult to correct the course since excuses and blame tend to accompany any attempt to analyze what went wrong.

We have learned to be particularly skeptical when plants tell us, for example, that all *new* documents will fall under the new system but *existing* documents will be converted on an as-needed basis. Usually this involves waiting until a particular document undergoes substantial change before moving it into the new format (and some documents seldom, if ever, undergo substantial change). Almost always, the users of the documents are short-changed under such a system. Change control cycle times increase, administrators become impatient with their internal customers, and sometimes the conversion is abandoned midstream.

There is, of course, no single formula for foolproof conversion. Nonetheless, if you are faced with the prospect of converting from one system to another, we strongly recommend that you pay special attention to avoiding overlong schedules. Be certain to account for the increased effort required to maintain duplicate systems and the potential effects on change control cycle time before making your decision. Consider brainstorming for creative ways to relieve the resource crunch. Here are a few suggestions:

- Poll your clerical personnel to see if some of them are willing, temporarily, to take on an additional assignment. Include people who do not normally interact with the administrative side of process discipline and use the conversion project as an opportunity to create interest and awareness.

- Overtime for those doing the work is a possibility, too, if your factory permits it. Sometimes this creates an enthusiastic pool of volunteers who can be trained, then can carry out their assignments outside their normal hours of work.

- Structure a work-study project as a partnership with a local high school or secretarial college.

- Inquire at an area community college or university whether or not interns are available to work with you to structure a project for which the intern(s) can receive official credit for successful completion of the project.

- Temporary service providers can provide advice about the cost and availability of part-time employees in your labor market. Sometimes this is quite reasonable, particularly if you can be flexible about the work hours.

- A newspaper ad might uncover plenty of people willing to work from home, telecommuting to complete the work after an on-site training session.

The point here is to take on the task of conversion, confident that there are creative ways to resolve the resource crunch and deliver a new, more robust, more user-friendly system even if the task looks impossible when you first consider it. Just be especially careful to construct your project so that your service providers clearly understand the formats and ground rules and that there are sufficient checkpoints to ensure that your requirements will be met.

One plant we know of completed a conversion from one system to another by first constructing a Pareto diagram of its most frequently used documents. They slated these for conversion first, and arranged to do the work on the 80 or 90 documents during a two-week summer shutdown. They found several clerical workers eager to work during shutdown in exchange for vacation at more convenient times for them and their families. The rest of the documents (there were about 350 in all) were converted during the next 10 months, using a well-organized schedule among the plant's clerical personnel.

Forms, Fields, and Filenames

An opposite situation arises when your enthusiasm for quickly converting to electronic systems causes you to shortchange the details that come back to haunt you later. Rather than risk having to redo your numbering scheme or live with unnecessarily complex access requirements, it is far more reasonable to spend time upfront carefully reviewing the decision rules and naming conventions before committing them to practice.

Taking into account the number of characters in a field, the structure of the input data and the order of entry on an electronic form can make the difference between a user-friendly system and one which is considered by its primary customers to be difficult or flawed. It makes good sense to check with the user community to validate the appropriateness of your decisions regarding design and content before you go forward with implementation. Remember that the output of the systems ought to be the primary rationale behind the input design.

This means that it is necessary to keep in mind what you will want to do with the data once it has been committed to electronic format. Let us say, for example, that you have decided to use the date format MMDDYY to create 011198 as a representation for January 11, 1998. This seems perfectly reasonable, and follows known conventions for assigning dates. It will likely be a whole year later when you realize that electronic sorting of the *date* field will interpose January 11, 1999, between January 11 and January 12, 1998. (The sorted strings for those three dates would be 011198, 011199, 011298.)

Similarly, let us say you decide to use an alphanumeric code for identifying experiments. You have assigned four-character alpha designations for each department (FORM for the forming department, FINI for the finishing department, INSP for the inspection department, and so on) and are going to append sequential numbers for the experiments based on which department originates them. You hope you will be able to sort on the experiment number field to provide each department manager a separate report. At the end of a three-month period, you have assigned only seven experiments, FORM1, FORM2, INSP1, FORM3, FORM4, FORM5, FINI1. So far, so good. At the end of a seven-month period, 27 experiments have been conducted; 13 of them originated by the forming department (and four of those took place just this month as part of bringing in a new piece of equipment). When you sort the data using the experiment number field, you discover that FORM1 is followed by FORM10, FORM11, FORM12, FORM13; then comes FORM2, FORM3, and so on. Now you have to rethink the experiment numbering scheme you have been using for eight months.

Both of these examples are taken from real-life situations. Fortunately, most of these kinds of problems can be avoided quite easily by involving information systems personnel in helping ensure good design. Simulation exercises to test designs with actual users will also aid in preventing disaster. If your organization is too small to have a separate information systems department, seek out internal or external resources that understand these issues and can help you avoid time-consuming and costly rework.

Robust and well-designed systems will accommodate years of growth before changes are required. They are worth the extra effort required to create them.

Enterprise Integration

Increasingly, large corporations are opting for enterprise-wide systems that integrate all aspects of data management. You will find that all such systems have a built-in assumption that the basic elements of process discipline are already in place. That is, provision is made for linking documents and the changes they undergo, materials can be associated with drawings and documents, and operator training can be captured and connected to correlate with other elements. Even experiment planning and results can be included as metadata and viewed online through associated software.

Because of the enormity of the task of re-creating the corporation's information management, these efforts are usually well funded and well staffed. That is the good news. The bad news turns out to be that a lack of discipline or consistency in inputting data will result in a crippled and ineffective behemoth that requires constant attention yet delivers little value. The long lead time to bring enterprise-wide data management into being gives you the opportunity to install process discipline as a prelude to realizing true value from the larger data system.

If you have the opportunity to participate in the early decision-making, be certain to take advantage of it so that you can anticipate its effect on what you hope to accomplish through process discipline. If you are in the process of installing process discipline concurrent with setting up an enterprise-wide data management system, then take the time to understand how to integrate your requirements with those of the larger system.

Do not allow yourself or your organization to become so enchanted with the possibilities of these comprehensive data treasure troves that you fail to distinguish between what the system can do given its inherent competency and what it *will* do given the realities of your own particular configuration.

Backups and Failsafes

Many people who have always worked under paper systems are uncomfortable with the notion of reliance on electronic technology. This is particularly true where operators are reluctant to depend on their computer screens because they do not understand what will happen if something goes wrong. They reason that if the computer provides work instructions, data input forms, and other key elements of day-to-day production information, they will not be able to continue to work if the screen goes blank.

Some plants insist on keeping up a paper file "just in case." This results in continuing the burden of distribution and administration which prompted moving to electronic technology in the first place. In truth, power outages do occur. Computer systems do crash unexpectedly. Screens do blink and then go blank. Local hardware can — and sometimes does — fail. So what can you do when these things happen?

The answer is no different from your reliance on automation in other parts of the process. When robotics first came into our factories, some Luddites argued that we ought to ensure our ongoing production by keeping redundant manual machines. If you had an automatic load cell for weighing product, there was a Pelouze scale in the back room waiting to rescue you when the new system failed. Got a new robot loader? Better keep that old handstacker "just in case."

It is true that these manual backups did come in handy once in a while, particularly in the pilot stages when performance was being fine-tuned. They are, however, redundant, and redundancy is inevitably expensive. It is also, except in very unusual cases, unnecessary. Better you should reread the section on maintenance management systems and treat electronic systems under the same ground rules. In other words, you ought to manage your electronic systems under approximately the same requirements as your automatic production machines. There is preventive maintenance to be scheduled, downtime records to be kept, and other aspects to be monitored and reported and managed.

What is important in this regard, however, is to ensure that your information systems personnel work with you to review the critical dependencies and provide appropriate electronic backup to tape or disk. Rational decisions as to the frequency of data backups can be made once the issues are understood.

CHAPTER 8

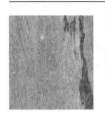

MANAGEMENT ISSUES

The Benefits of Process Discipline

When an operation is run under strong process discipline, several excellent things occur:

1. Just by becoming consistent, by getting personnel to agree on the one best way to run a particular step in the operation, writing it down, and training all to operate that way, the variability of that step is reduced and some problems and their related losses and defects disappear. You may not know the individual cause(s) and effect(s), or even that they happened, but making the entire operation consistent raises yields and reduces quality problems simply from variability reduction. Many problems have their own origin in deviations from the best-known practice; elimination of these, of course, is part of the improvement from variability reduction.

2. Since consistency provides you with a lower noise manufacturing operation, that operation becomes a much more fruitful test bed for observation, experimentation, learning, and improvement. Any data collected on the process are less contaminated with unexplained variation, so analysis

is easier to do and meaningful trends are easier to identify. Experiments can be run with smaller sample sizes and fewer replications, and the results will still be more reliable.

Engineers would say that the signal-to-noise ratio has been increased, and therefore, relationships become more obvious. In practical terms, it means that problems can be solved more quickly, and that *process learning and improvement proceeds at a faster rate.*

3. Process discipline makes use of two fundamental feedback systems to prevent the process from drifting off consistent standard operation. The first is frequent (usually daily) audit to assure that all controllable variables are running within recommended ranges. The second is the use of process information systems which provide frequent, accurate reporting, by item, of yields, rates, losses by defect, downtime by cause, and numbers of parts processed at each step.

This combined feedback enables operating people to identify any newly arising problems early and to act quickly to diagnose and fix them. These systems also allow us to track progress on problems being "cured," to make sure that the corrective action underway is really working. The joint effect of the feedback loops is to protect against deterioration, and to assure the success of continuing improvement.

4. Process discipline makes excellent use of the preventive systems that most plants already have (often in some state of disrepair). Examples of such systems include maintenance management, calibration, production information, material management, statistical process control, tooling control, and incoming and final inspection.

In general, these systems have been developed to prevent known problems from arising, to protect the customer, and to maintain uninterrupted stable operation. When competently implemented, these systems make the operation perform at or near its best capability. For instance, if we consider the impact of excellently maintained production equipment on product quality, uptime, capacity, and cost, it becomes clear that these systems are basic to top-level operation.

5. When utilizing change control and experimentation, we bring to bear both the scientific method and the science of statistics in support of process improvement. Using both competently, our decision-making becomes as good as it can be for the facts available.

6. The flow chart has shown the most appropriate sequence of actions to maximize the rate of process improvement. We have seen that process discipline actions should be taken first, so that gains can be "locked in" as they are made. This minimizes what we have termed "recidivism."

It is disheartening to see how often manufacturing people solve the same problems over and over again because of the lack of systems to capture learning, to maintain it in accessible memory, and to assure that it is in constant use.

Fifteen Specific Examples

Process discipline improves yields, allows process improvement to go faster, provides early warning of nascent problems, tracks progress on corrective actions underway, prevents many problems from occurring, enables the operation to run in stable, uninterrupted fashion at close to its basic capability, makes use of science and statistics for decisions on the process, and institutionalizes and consolidates gains you achieve so they become permanent.

Now that we have summarized the impacts of process discipline on manufacturing *operation*, let us review actual examples of how it has affected manufacturing *performance*.

Profit — and Lots More of It

CASE 1

A wonderful new housewares product was started up in a plant after several years of difficult development by a committed team of hands-on process experts. The charismatic leader of the group insisted that only his artist-craftsmen could make this process run, and so they personally called the shots around the clock, upstream and downstream, seven days a week.

After two years, the product was a great market success, but barely broke even financially. Whenever the plant people were allowed to take control of the operation, things got worse, reinforcing the position of the charismatic leader. The company was considering eliminating the product line, because there was no return on a heavy capital investment, and the market needed a wider line that required still more investment.

As a last resort, a new plant manager who believed wholeheartedly in process discipline was appointed. He insisted that the best-known method of operation be documented and the process run that way by the plant's operators. The development leader challenged the decision up to the chairman, lost, and took an extended leave of absence.

In the succeeding 18 months, the process yields went from mid-40s to mid-80s, the product line became the most profitable in the company, the plant was expanded, and hundreds of millions of parts were sold. That plant ran under increasingly stringent process discipline until the plant manager was promoted.

CASE 2

A foreign subsidiary of a multinational corporation made a component for an older model of a major appliance (which fit the market in its region). The domestic plant, which had transferred this important item to make capacity available for the next model, had run the item with yields in the upper 70s after years of experience. The subsidiary, noted for the energy and manufacturing capabilities of its country's people, was in serious trouble as its yields stagnated at 55%. The operation was running at a loss.

A domestic manager with deep knowledge of process discipline visited, toured the plant, and then met with the local management group. He told them (through sentence-by-sentence interpretation) that if the current results did not change, it was his opinion that their factory would close. He also explained process discipline, and said he believed that the plant had substantial potential to improve even beyond the results of the domestic plant if process discipline were implemented rapidly and thoroughly.

He sent a knowledgeable person (a native of that country) there for several weeks to train them in process discipline, and watched their yields rise to 88% over the next 11 months, while their profitability exceeded all targets ever envisioned for that plant by a wide margin.

CASE 3

A large plant was one of the few remaining domestic operations in an industry that had almost entirely migrated overseas where costs were lower and quality was considered better. Since its start-up decades ago, it had operated in a traditional mode, with few systems and procedures, and ad hoc decisions made on the advice of experienced area "gurus." The plant's financial performance, under pressure from well-managed competitors, eroded almost every year, and it seemed inevitable that it would not survive.

A new plant manager unfamiliar with this business was brought in, and he took some time to decide on a new strategy. Unsurprisingly, he decided on process discipline, but he realized that the entire culture of the plant required changing. The plant manager brought in customers to address his employees, and they were told their prices and quality put them at the bottom of the preferred supplier list. He patiently and quietly promoted the need for a change in culture, and placed increasing emphasis on total implementation of process discipline.

The plant's profitability has climbed steadily, exceeding profitability goals for the first times in years. It has undergone several expensive expansions, and is competing successfully for business against overseas competitors, bringing long lost volume back to the United States.

CASE 4

A plant had several different product lines serving a "cyclical" industry. The business was profitable when the volume was strong, and struggled to break even during the slumps. It was decided to build a new plant in another state for the largest product line.

The enlightened new management instituted process discipline in all modes from the very start. The plant was profitable in its first month of operation, exceeding the highest margins ever previously seen after three months, and was running at 90% gross margin on incremental volume after seven months. The plant became a money machine that ignored the "cyclical" nature of the business. Three of the plant's four top people were promoted before the first year ended.

Vastly Improved Product Quality

Suppose you had to make a drastic improvement to your products' quality to meet customer requirements or new government regulations. What would you do? If you thought things through carefully, analyzed your own and other people's historical successes, and embarked on a program to achieve lasting improvements, you would proceed with process discipline. That is what it was devised for.

CASE 5

A plant, whose main product line was packaging for pharmaceutical materials, was notified that tiny fragments of its packaging material occasionally would find their way into the drug, and potentially into the patient. Although the incidence was rare, the customer (appropriately) regarded this as a major problem, and demanded that it be quickly resolved. The customer took this opportunity to inform the plant that several other of its quality parameters were also below acceptable limits, that its overall performance was the lowest of suppliers of these items, and that it had a short time to correct the problem or be dropped as a supplier.

Over protests of, "It's not true; nothing has changed;" and "We can't afford to retool the line with entirely new equipment;" and "Their standards are unreasonable;" an internal fact-finding team studied the plant's and competitors' materials and determined that the customer's comments were true. Division management rejected arguments to either invest in a new manufacturing line or to give up the business.

Instead, an intensive and competently led process discipline campaign was undertaken. The objective was to run an extremely consistent process, and to find and eliminate all sources of fragmentation. One year later, the plant was told it had the best quality of all suppliers, and that information was used to negotiate a sole source supplier contract with the customer.

CASE 6

A plant made precision mechanical components from brittle materials for many of the largest, most famous and most demanding corporations in the world. The plant's products functioned satisfactorily in their customers' applications, but the finished appearance of their products was visibly inferior to those of their largest competitor, a well-known Asian company.

The domestic plant's overall performance as a vendor, considering price, delivery, flexibility on changes, and response to new product needs was superior, but several customers indicated that the competitor would be given increasing market share unless the product appearance became at least equivalent.

The plant embarked on a tightened process discipline program while it did development work on advanced finishing techniques and equipment. The process discipline program yielded such improved results that most of the finishing development plans were shelved. The domestic plant ended up getting higher market share than it had before the issue arose, even in the competitor's home region.

CASE 7

The plant discussed as Case 3 in the "Profit..." section above needed a total culture change and invited customer executives to "lay it on the line" at internal meetings. This plant started its process discipline program with most of its quality measures at the bottom of the list. Their process discipline program was *primarily* aimed at quality improvement. While profitability improved, quality did so simultaneously. This joint rise occurs almost all the time. This plant became equal to the best of its competitors, quality-wise.

Predictability and On-Time Delivery

The authors knew a vice president of manufacturing who said, "I'd much rather have a plant that had 50 ± 2 % yields than one that had 60 ± 25 % yields. With the first plant, I can plan, I can meet customer delivery promises, I can control staffing sensibly, I can control inventories, and I can run my business. Even though the second plant has higher overall yields, I can't do any of those things, I am constantly embarrassed and harassed, and my business is out of control." This executive was one of the strongest advocates of process discipline for obvious reasons. *Variability is the enemy of manufacturing predictability, and manufacturing predictability is the cornerstone of manufacturing control.*

CASE 8

A new product line based on a proprietary, newly developed coating for conventional products came through market testing very successfully. The division decided to build a minimalist, short construction time, low-cost factory that would demonstrate that conventional "frills" such as documentation, measuring instruments, control systems, maintenance groups, quality control, etc., could be dispensed with or have several of them handled by one person. The plant was started up under an aggressive cheerleading manager.

After about four months, yields on this deceptively simple four-step process were around 40%, uptime was about 40%, receipts of good product were grossly inadequate to service the "successful" market introduction, and reject parts were being shipped to another state for an expensive rework operation requiring heavy equipment not available in the new plant.

A process discipline team was sent to the new plant which was bleeding losses, but which was still not supporting the "successful" market introduction with enough parts to sell. The team quickly identified the need for infrastructure, and for attitude change to "do it right the first time by the numbers." It took nine months to build the infrastructure (there was no production report, no maintenance responsibility, no documentation, no standard setups) and get to 90% yields, 90% uptime, no rework, and an operation that ran in control and supplied all needed product profitably (and whose results continued to improve under the permanent staff). What the team did was classic process discipline; most of which could have been operative at startup. The cheerleader took early retirement.

CASE 9

A technically advanced, rather sophisticated medical instrument was introduced into production at a plant that was successfully manufacturing other, simpler products for the medical market. This plant was already operating under the Food and Drug Administration's (FDA) Good Manufacturing Practices (GMP) guidelines, which are related to process discipline. However, in the years of running simpler products, the system disciplines had deteriorated, and the plant's controls were sometimes given lip service.

When throughput times grew very large, and good salable instruments rarely exited the production line, management requested help. A quick study showed that although seven workdays were required to complete a unit if there were no problems, the median completion time was 48 days. Not one completed instrument worked as designed; all required expensive rework. Further, some units never became good instruments, and ended up being cannibalized for parts.

Observation showed that the production and engineering groups had developed a mindset of assembling quickly, sending it into test, and depending on rework to handle any shortcomings. When it became clear that not enough units were being completed, *the practice of moving things through the line before completing a workstation's required actions and test was accelerated, making things much worse.* The plant staff was shocked to hear that analysis of their recent data showed that the average instrument was going into "final test" eight times!

Once the issue was identified, it was apparent that units had to receive complete assembly and thorough test as specified at each workstation, that repeating problems had to be analyzed until root causes were identified and fixed, and that thorough process discipline (even when seemingly slower) was far preferable to fast, furious, and uncontrolled processing. In a matter of weeks, typical throughput time had been reduced to 10 days.

CASE 10

Wonderfully good results of process discipline can sometimes lead to problems when those good results are unexpected, and not planned for, and when necessary action has not been taken far enough in advance.

In a new plant where process discipline was implemented comprehensively and extremely well, results far exceeded any experience on this product line in its previous location. It turned out that for the numbers of units started and people on the factory floor, about 40% more good parts were being receipted than had been expected after six months operation.

The continuing fast increase in yields caught management by surprise, and sales and marketing were not afforded sufficient lead time for special promotions, price reductions, or other actions to gain market share and use the newly available capacity.

So the sad result was a significant layoff, people moving to different jobs and requiring new training, and reduced yields for a time until the newly allocated workforce was thoroughly familiar with their jobs. And it is always more difficult to motivate people to improve operations after this kind of experience.

Keener observation and faster reaction could have saved much of the pain, and may even have given the organization a chance to dramatically build its competitive position in the business.

Easier, Faster Road to Improvement

We mentioned previously that process discipline imparts a higher signal-to-noise ratio to the process, making relationships more obvious and allowing process learning to proceed at a faster rate.

And, there is much less backsliding in a process with strong process discipline, so less time and effort has to be spent catching back up to previously achieved levels.

Since process discipline contains a wide variety of tools from different technical specialties, from time to time one of these becomes an important Eureka! with major positive impact, even though it is a common tactic in other fields. Two examples follow:

CASE 11

A large multiproduct corporation acquired a recent startup company making high-speed chip devices from exotic semiconductor materials. A high proportion of the acquired company's personnel held doctorates, and they naturally presumed that volume manufacturing of the devices meant many of the doctoral personnel should be building them in parallel on lab benches. Since the efforts were individual, each device builder (researcher) reported production results only on completed devices that underwent final test.

A veteran manufacturing engineering manager was dispatched from the parent company to provide assistance. He proposed instituting a production report summarizing the combined efforts of all device builders, and showing how many units had reached each intermediate level of fabrication, what the losses were, and where and why they occurred. At first, there was widespread objection to this reporting, because the researchers did not want their "exploratory" activity results shown; they felt it would inhibit their willingness to innovate, and would make apparent the problems they were encountering in fabrication.

But, when they had been convinced to try reporting as an "experiment," they soon realized that a much more informative picture of manufacturing status and the nature and severity of the problems emerged. They welcomed the new "technical advance" of the production report, and soon requested many enhancements.

At this point, the veteran manager felt ready to address the issue of whether personnel with doctorates individually building devices on lab benches was really the preferred method of manufacturing.

CASE 12

An important (to its parent company) complex manufacturing plant covered a long straight-line distance, and had basement and mezzanine operations in addition. In trying to institute process discipline in what had been a somewhat loosely controlled operation, the widespread geography proved to be a barrier, since supervisors often claimed they simply "could not cover the ground."

Someone suggested that a capable technician should be assigned as a daily auditor of the entire process. This was done, and this individual soon established a route, and acquired a clipboard and forms, and a variety of instruments and tools. He started his rounds each morning at 6:00 A.M., checked whether each of 440 variables were in or out of allowable ranges, recorded the information, and distributed copies of the exception report to the attendees of the 9:00 A.M. production meeting. In a few months, typical daily out-of-range "exceptions" were reduced from 10% to 2%, and yields showed a steep gain.

Business Longevity

Why does process discipline give firms a much better chance to survive for many decades?

- The data-based decision-making protocols of process discipline greatly reduce the likelihood that the firm could make unfortunate process decisions that lead to major losses, or even to its immediate demise.

- Consistency improves yields, prevents quality upsets, affords faster improvement, captures learning to maintain stability at high levels, and assists in meeting delivery commitments. These all serve to keep an enterprise in a strong competitive position, and make it probable that the company can be a leader likely to survive normal business vicissitudes.

These advantages will not overcome being a buggy whip manufacturer when automobiles take over, sticking with designs based on obsolete technology such as not converting products to computer control, or maintaining prices so high that they become an umbrella inviting in competitors.

But, as these two examples illustrate, consistently excellent manufacturing can extend the life of businesses:

CASE 13

An electronic component was developed for the guidance and control system of a key missile. It was forecast that the product life would be five years and that there would be minimal market for replacements or spares.

Seven years after major procurement started, a long slow volume decline began, but after *an additional 15 years*, sales volume was still substantial, and profit even more so. This superb product was manufactured under meticulous process discipline that was required by the initial customer. It was subsequently designed into other systems, used by other customers, and purchased by other countries with U.S. government support.

CASE 14

A pollution control product was introduced to meet new federal requirements. This product life was expected to be limited to five years, because it was widely predicted that the product would be supplanted by newer, better technology. More than 20 years after introduction, the business is larger than ever, and services a worldwide market. Manufacturing and product development proceeded so effectively under strong process discipline that new technologies have not yet been able to displace the product.

Reduced Capital Expenditure

There are many uses for capital. Some have good underlying reasons, and some do not.

Good applications include new products, expansion of business for existing products, and investments in better technology such as instruments, computers, or machinery.

Examples of "bad" applications are such things as buying additional equipment to compensate for poorer yields than if the process was run in control, or trying to solve periodic process problems of unidentified origin with new capital investment. These "bad" demands for capital can almost always be avoided by good process discipline.

Competitive Advantage

CASE 15

A new invention was moved into pilot production and then into full-scale manufacture with major emphasis on process discipline, right from the start, and continuing thereafter.

Competition, from some of the largest, most technically capable and financially strong of the world's companies (who quickly copied the invention), was brutally aggressive. Nevertheless, the originator gradually moved from being new to the business into an equal position with the leading suppliers. Ten years after introduction, this company held the largest market share, which it is continuing to increase, even though several of the competitors had large internal markets.

In this situation, process discipline was used as a strategy and a weapon, and it helped the organization to achieve a pre-eminent position. This group has publicly declared that process discipline deserves much of the credit for its success.

Process Capability Improvement

Achieving Process Capability Improvement

Process capability improvement (PCI) means making fundamental changes to the process, or replacing and upgrading all or part of the current equipment/process, or adding to it in a way that makes a significant positive change to the performance of the process.

PCI can be accomplished in a very diverse set of ways. What differentiates this group of actions from those that aim at consistency and those that attack assignable cause problems to bring the process into statistical control is that PCI involves fundamental change(s) to the process and/or materials and equipment.

The things you do to achieve consistency are focused on **running the current process as singularly as possible**. The work to bring the process into statistical control is targeted at finding and fixing those few things that prevent a process that has consistent inputs from having consistent outputs. The objective is to **make the process you have run as well as it can (or to achieve its full capability)**.

Since PCI requires fundamental improvement to the process, and since we have already noted that PCI is usually capital-intensive, and is almost always skill-intensive, it is obvious that PCI comes at a price, and sometimes a stiff one. In general, you must invest skilled people's time and capital, two scarce resources, to derive the benefits of PCI. And, in general, PCI requires long lead times before you realize its advantages and can take them to the bank.

Evaluating What Getting PCI Will Require

Usually, then, the first questions you need to ask are:

1. Are we realizing the full potential of the process we have by running it in statistical control? (New equipment and/or a new process are often the panacea for a less-than-optimum process.)

2. If we are close to statistical control, or could get there, would the best-run current process be adequate to meet business goals and competitive requirements?

3. What are our best estimates of the cost of achieving our goals each way (running the current process the best it can be run versus a new PCI process), and how long do we expect it to take each way?

4. If we opt for the PCI route and we are not running our current process as well as we can, will the new process be built on sand, and be limited or disabled by the variabilities and weaknesses of the surrounding parts of the existing process, or the limitations of current plant systems?

5. If those current process weaknesses will limit the performance of the PCI system and increase the risk of not achieving its promised results, do we need to improve the current process by bringing it into statistical control **as well as** invest in the new PCI process? And must our resource and time estimates be based on both goals?

In our experience, fair-minded, competent and experienced people can do a good job answering most of these questions if not pressured by some upper management bias. Question three is the exception. Those who recommend new processes are naturally biased in their favor, and that preference is reinforced by the glamour and excitement of the new and technically more advanced PCI route as opposed to the grind-it-out nature of optimizing the familiar old known methods. The risks of timing and performance of the new system are classically underestimated — in Dr. Samuel Johnson's famous words, "the triumph of hope over experience." The only (and admittedly tepid) antidote we know is close questioning of the proposal estimates, and reference to the recent history of such forecasts' accuracy.

Keeping Focused on Primary Objectives

All this having been said and carefully examined, when the decision for capability improvement has been made, many things must be considered. First, there are numerous real and potential drivers for capability improvement — increased capacity, reduced cost, tighter tolerances, better product performance, additional product features, greater flexibility, improved raw material utilization, compliance with new or pending legislation, and others. Although the decision to go after PCI is usually driven primarily by one of these issues, by the time project planning is completed, you frequently end up aiming for several or even many of them, and that usually seems to make strategic sense. After all, if you are doubling your capacity, you certainly want that increment to be lower in manufacturing cost, more flexible, and to have other advantages you may need.

However, you must recognize that each additional feature increases cost, complexity, and risk, and this is especially so when new technology not in previous commercial use is introduced. At this point, you have to start making the hard decisions about how much complexity and risk you should be willing to take on. Again, most technical project leaders will represent that risk increases, at most, linearly with the number of targeted goals. However, historical evidence reveals that difficulties actually increase exponentially, even under the best conditions.

These comments are not based on "experienced observation" or anecdotal evidence; they are based on a series of research studies done by the Rand Corporation for the U.S. Department of Energy (Understanding Cost Growth and Performance Shortfalls in Pioneer Process Plants), whose conclusions were as follows:

1. Earliest cost estimates averaged less than one half of actual costs.

2. The assumptions that planners make about the accuracy and uncertainty of their capital cost estimates are frequently unrealistic, and not only biased low, but also so uncertain they cannot be relied upon at all.

3. The major problems come not from external influences such as inflation or regulatory changes, but from low levels of process and project understanding.

4. The average plant only operated at 63% of design capacity eight months after startup. Expectations were 85% six months after startup.

The data come from work admittedly performed on processes involving some new technology, but the projects were done by some of the largest and most capable U.S. companies including, among others, Air Products and Chemicals, ARCO Chemical, Dow Chemicals, du Pont, Exxon, 3M, Mobil, Rohm & Haas, and Texaco.

The message is "Let the authorizers beware." Another message is "Keep it simple."

PCI in a Process Discipline Environment

In a process discipline environment, the first considerations should be "Have we achieved a high level of consistency?" and "Have we solved the great majority of 'assignable cause' type problems so that the process is running at or close to its capability?" Until you can answer those two questions positively, you should not yet be investing time, money, and effort on PCI (except in quite unusual circumstances). On the other hand, when those two questions can be answered affirmatively, the probability is much higher that PCI will be successful.

Developing and Implementing the Program

When the decision is made to proceed with PCI, a highly competent technologist who knows how to learn the totality of business needs should be selected (perhaps leading a team if the project is large). This individual must search out all the internal and external options in a realistic and open-minded way, trying to find the most economical, reliable, simple, capable way to improve the process in ways most congruent with business needs. The proposal must also be within the investment capabilities of the firm, must meet the financial "hurdle rate," and should have some ability to be modified for future utility. Of course, it must be equal to or better than all known competitive capability. It should be from a supplier who delivers high quality equipment and/or instrumentation on time and within budget. The equipment should be easy to install, start up, maintain, and train people on. The description of this assignment is one of the reasons major capital investments are made infrequently.

A small group of key players should meet frequently with the technology leader to review the program from technology, economic, market, and risk perspectives. The group should arrive at a consensus on the final version of the proposal and capital appropriation. When defining the financial benefits, the group should be sure to think broadly about such things as reduced working capital, improved market share and competitive position, better manufacturing predictability and customer service, reduced downtime and work-in-process inventory, etc. Accountants will determine discounted cash flow to four significant figures (when uncertainties limit statistical validity to one significant figure) but contributions should be welcomed. Just remember that three or four years hence, the appropriation request will probably be audited against what actually happened.

Caveats for PCI Implementation

The leader of the project needs to remember:

- Everything unexpected that occurs has a detrimental effect on cost and schedule.

- If 99% of the system is good, you are in real trouble. Manufacturing systems fail at the weakest link. Keep working to find out where that is, and how to strengthen it.

- Allow for many things to go wrong when you make out the final schedule. They will not, but other things you never dreamed of will go wrong. You will need all the slack, and then some.

- Plan and budget right from the start for the documentation, the training, the other process discipline systems, and the time to implement them and to get them working right. Never compromise those dollars and that time although you surely will be pressured to.

- Keep smiling. The startup may turn your hair white, but, if the new process really works, it will probably last longer and make more money than ever imagined.

Liability in a Litigious Environment

No matter how small your company or apparently innocuous the products you make, once you engage in commercial production you become liable for the consequences of your manufacturing decision-making. Your vulnerability is manifested each time a headline, newscast, or magazine cover blares out the tidings of another product recall. Let a plane fall from the Florida sky, a Chicago toddler ingest a loose component from a cuddly teddy bear, or a woman in Denver contract dermatitis and our nation's manufacturers examine their collective conscience. Could your own processes withstand the withering scrutiny of a panel of industry experts called in to examine your maintenance records, question your employees, and investigate your manufacturing practices?

Process discipline is perhaps the cheapest form of liability insurance. When you can demonstrate that you have used the collective knowledge of your entire workforce to document the best way to make your products, that you train your workforce to follow documented procedures, that you audit frequently, control process change, and conduct careful experiments, you vastly improve the likelihood that 12 citizens will decide that you have fulfilled your obligations to a consuming public.

You cannot guarantee that instilling process discipline in your own operations will obviate your need for liability insurance. Juries are unpredictable entities at best, and lawyers are paid to discover and exploit the weaknesses of their opponents. Nonetheless, process discipline certainly will lessen the probability that defective products will enter the stream of commerce in the first place, and mightily will increase your chances of prevailing if ever your manufacturing practices are challenged in a court of law. Experience also tells us that, even if you cannot completely escape culpability, awards are always lower when you establish your defense on the due diligence of process discipline.

An Easter-weekend fire destroyed the newly built residence of a family of four while they attended church services several miles away. Suit was brought against the manufacturer of the self-cleaning oven recently installed in the ultramodern kitchen. The case presented included details of the family's pizza supper the previous evening and the wife's decision to put the oven into self-clean mode just before departing for church. The homeowners hoped to recover sufficient damages to rebuild their under-insured dwelling. (They had transferred the insurance from their previous house and had not yet increased the amount of their coverage to account for the difference in value between the two residences.)

While many factors ultimately convinced the jury that the oven was not itself the cause of the fire, the chief counsel for the company used this example to illustrate how successful defense rests heavily on establishing an image of a prudent, conscientious manufacturer who operates under process discipline. Now retired, he told us that he always began his case preparation by visiting the manufacturing plant and investigating how strong their systems were. Strong systems (including process flow charts, standard operating procedures, change control and experiment results, and training and audit records) provided him with the bulk of the information he required to simply and elegantly guide the jury to a successful conclusion.

Defending a major multinational corporation in a case involving serious burns to a child under 12, corporate attorneys relied heavily on process documentation to demonstrate the care with which the allegedly defective appliance was manufactured. In addition, daily audit records were used to show that the product in question was made under conditions consistent with thousands of other units which were manufactured during the same period and which were defect-free. Training records documented that production workers and inspectors were well qualified to recognize and eliminate defects from the process stream. Despite the horrible nature of the evidence (pictures taken immediately after the accident and the scarred victim's presence in the courtroom many months later), the jury determined that the company had manufactured its products reliably and responsibly and was not culpable for the boy's injuries.

Isn't This Bureaucracy, and Won't It Cost Me My Competitiveness?

If you put structure and procedures into your operations, won't that constrain your flexibility and innovation? Won't bureaucratic thickets slow you down and limit your competitive capabilities?

Let us explore the appropriate balance between the routine and the ad hoc.

Systematic Operation

Consider the way a business organization deals with several situations:

1. Process a group of incoming orders.
2. Run an intricate multistep manufacturing operation.
3. Track and control inventories.
4. Invoice customers, and follow up on the slow payers.

Most people would agree that there should be a defined, structured way that each of these situations should be handled. They would agree that the responsible person performing this activity should not be free to *reinvent the process, ad hoc, as the activity proceeds*. These situations should be routine; they are repeated often, and are complex enough that they interact with and impact other systems and groups inside and outside the organization. What might happen, for instance, in processing a new order, if you allowed a rookie sales service person to innovate a new set of requested information from the customer, to select new destinations for each piece of information, and to extemporize commitments to the customer? The very thought generates migraines.

You know that systems like the one for handling incoming orders have undergone continuous evolution and improvement over the years to correct omissions and take into account the requirements of the many interested parties who need to know some or all of the information available about this order. You also know that you are unlikely to be able to quickly identify, offhand, all these "receivers" and their specific needs.

We suggest that this class of business activities should come under the heading "systematic operation," meaning they are repetitive, too important to permit frequent error, too complicated or intricate to be fully visualized quickly, and you do not want to have to figure out how to do it right again each time. You must

analyze the situation and capture all the needed actions in procedures, computer programs, videotapes, drawings, etc., and then
you try hard to do it this way all the time. This "bureaucracy" benefits you every day, and the better you do it, the greater the benefits. If you design it well the first time, make corrections as needed,
and keep it updated as the business needs change, you should be
proud of it, because it will save a lot of money and trouble.

Ad Hoc Reactive

Now let us consider how the business organization deals with
several different situations:

1. The secret new product plans for the next 30 months,
   together with the associated advance drawings, have
   apparently been stolen by a disgruntled former employee.
   Her friends say she is now in China.
2. The company's only gizmo plant, and the regional sales
   office that shares its building in Des Moines, Iowa, burned
   to the ground.
3. A coup in a foreign country has created an opportunity to
   run that country's communications, highway, and rail systems, but the U.S. State Department is negative.
4. The Mobile, Alabama, plant, which manufactures the key
   intermediate for the most profitable product line, has been
   told that its large neighbor desperately needs that space,
   and would pay a fortune for it.

Most people would agree that these issues should be handled
on an "ad hoc reactive" individual basis. There does not seem to
be anything repetitive or routine, and any prior experience probably has only limited applicability. This is not to say you should
not analyze and plan, but that when you do, you start with a clean
sheet rather than use as a model something you are now doing or
have done before.

Notice our thesis that the need for structure (or not) funda-
mentally depends on the nature of the activity, and that just about

all manufacturing (except maybe that of the artist-craftsman) belongs in the "systematic operation" column.

Gray Situations

Of course, we have simplified the discussion by picking the black and white ones and avoiding the gray situations. Our recommendation is not to treat the gray ones as "ad hoc reactive," in spite of how strong the bias against "bureaucracy" may be. Instead, we say to break the gray ones into their black and white segments, and to treat the segments appropriately. When that is done, a gray activity may have several of its parts structured and procedurized, and several left to be handled as "ad hoc reactive."

For example, suppose an incoming order arrives for one of our units, but with some special customization required. You would process the order in our "systematic" mode with information flowing to all the normal recipients, but you would describe the unique custom aspects in some detailed "ad hoc" manner with special information flow.

Preventive Synthesis

The above analysis seems logical and sensible (to us) and shows the extremes of the spectrum of needs for structure. But, if organizations followed those precepts alone, even if they did them quite well, probably few would survive very long. Organizations need to learn, to adapt, and to change. They must be able to review the things that have happened in their businesses and ask, "What could we have done in advance to be better prepared for this situation?" and "What actions should we be taking from now on so the negative events will be less painful and we can take better advantage of the opportunities?" and "What do other best companies do that we can apply to our business?" and, even, "Our current quotation system is too cumbersome and too slow for us to be leaders—how can it be improved?" And they must take action on these issues. Often, this action is synthesizing preventive systems.

The name is probably too fancy for the activity. For instance, a decision may be made to extend fire insurance to include business interruption coverage. Storage of certain critical spare parts or raw materials may be purposely dispersed to reduce vulnerability. Suppliers may be told to keep a limited supply of spares or product "on consignment" in your plants to protect against sudden shutdown. Security procedures may be tightened to avoid repeating the loss of intellectual property or of precious metals. A contingency plan may be developed for a 10-day power outage, or for the approach of a hurricane. Of course, the most important one is a campaign to institute process discipline throughout manufacturing.

To improve faster than their competitors and to last for the long term, organizations must develop the feedback loop that starts with relentless review of their recent history and ends with implementation of preventive or improvement mechanisms. They need to install mechanisms or systems so that rather than just responding to the present problem, recurrence of the problem is prevented.

To evaluate whether a particular preventive system is worth developing is straightforward. The system's expected value is the product of (the probability the event could occur, in say 10 years), times (the cost if the event happens), times (the fraction of that cost which could be avoided by the preventive system). For example, let us consider developing a contingency plan for the approach of a hurricane that would damage the Galveston plant. The probability of that occurring in the next 10 years might be .25 or 25%. The cost of damage without the contingency plan might be four million dollars. Perhaps the contingency plan might enable you to avoid 60% of the loss. The benefit (or expected value) of the contingency plan would be .25 x $4,000,000 x .6 = $600,000. The chances are that a contingency plan could be developed for much less than that, so, if the three estimates are valid, this preventive system would be well worth establishing.

Sounds Good, But in My Plant...

Process discipline "aims to achieve consistency ... to assure that each *product* manufactured is identical" and strives to accomplish this by documenting the process, training the people to the document, auditing the process to assure it is being run as documented, and strictly controlling change. These all are structure and procedure.

When it is proposed to institute process discipline, the most frequent avoidance responses are:

1. We depend on the skill and judgment of our experienced people. That is why we hire good people.

2. Our strategy is to capture all of this on computer so we are not dependent on people.

3. Specifying in detail how the process should run stifles people's innovation.

4. This company's high-tech environment is too fast-paced to develop and follow all of these procedures.

5. We despise and avoid bureaucracy here. We want no staff organizations, no documents gathering dust, and no quality T-shirts.

Al Smith, a 1928 presidential candidate, once said, "No matter how you slice it, it's still baloney!" Some specific comments on these alibis:

1. Your skilled and experienced people have zero turnover, never get sick, and all do it exactly alike ... or do they?

2. The computer does job changes, maintenance, troubleshoots problems, lubricates the equipment, and notices when output quality starts deteriorating, or does it?

3. Do you allow people to experiment on the process and make changes without valid confirming data? Do they ever communicate which changes they have introduced?

4. "If you don't have time to do it right, you'll have plenty of time to do it over." Whoever said that knew a lot about manufacturing. These systems and rules are the strategy

that gets it done right the fastest. Their use avoids lost time (and poorer quality to the customer) for finding the new problems which arise from actions which have not been thoroughly pretested, diagnosing the causes, and getting back to the starting point, before making any progress at all.

5. There are no T-shirts, the documents do not gather any dust, and the staff organization is one person, but management, technical people, and operators will have to allocate some time to process discipline. This allocation of time is an investment that will eliminate midnight phone calls, quality upsets, and low yield epidemics, and will result in steadily increasing gross margins. The primary danger is it will get the successful people promoted out of the factory.

6. While the nature of the manufacturing activity demands a lot of structure, there are significant costs incurred for implementing structure, and there are dangers from not doing it well or misapplying it. Documentation and training must be done competently, effectively, and to appropriate depth. The best knowledge of key people (including operators) must be solicited and incorporated. Operating people must feel ownership and control of the procedures and the rules, or they won't abide by them. All systems must be kept current with the process. You should not apply total effort to processes that are still developmental and unstable, or where customers keep changing their requirements at rates that indicate they still do not know what they need. Competent and enlightened leadership of the process discipline effort is essential. It is a role for a mature and successful manager, not someone who has not succeeded at other responsibilities.

Summary

Structure, procedure, and system are appropriate for certain activities and not for others. They are necessities for excellent manufacturing. Would you want to fly from New York to Paris in a plane whose engines and control systems were made by processes that were improvised by the assembly crew?

CHAPTER 9

ASSOCIATED TECHNOLOGY SYSTEMS

Production Information Systems

Production information systems that are accurate, provide the important information about an operation, fully account for the disposition of the materials and parts entering the operation, and include certain details we shall enumerate, are essential to successful manufacturing. They become the primary feedback systems that tell you how well the operation is working, where the areas are that need improvement, and how successful your previous actions to fix problems have been. They enable you to quickly identify and attack those weaknesses that inevitably arise in plant activities. With good information, you can pinpoint potential difficulties in their earliest phases, still close in location and time to their root causes. You do not have to search problems out after they have grown, taken on different coloration, and meandered downstream.

The main information element in most plants is the production report. Also important in most operations are quality reports — incoming, final, and in-process including statistical process control charts and cusum charts; maintenance management reports; and various others usually focusing on inventories and production scheduling. In this chapter, our primary attention will be devoted to the production report, usually the most important and informative. A plant with a good production report is usually well managed, and there is some likelihood that its manufacturing is in control. A plant without a good production report has rarely been well managed, and it is not often that its manufacturing is in control.

Essential Elements of a Production Report

In almost all cases, production reports should be based on actual numbers of parts processed (where the majority of products are discrete), or actual pounds or tons or kilograms where the product is produced as a process stream. The report should show the actual numbers of parts into and out of each operation step, and of the entire operation, for the time unit covered (often one day, but sometimes a week or even one shift). The report *should not be based on accounting standards; performance to those standards may be shown, but should never be used for analysis or problem solving.* (The reason for not using accounting standards for analysis is that they have assumptions and expectations built into them that often are incorrect or imprecise, although they may have been the best guesses that could be made when the standards were formulated.)

The good pieces (or pounds) produced divided by the total pieces into an operation step is called the yield. Likewise, the good pieces out of an entire manufacturing operation divided by the total pieces into that operation is the yield for the entire operation. An alternate method of calculating yield for an entire operation is to multiply the percentage yields at each operation step all together. This is often called the cumulative yield or the multiplied yield of the total operation. These two ways of calculating yield for an overall operation have different advantages and applications. The cumulative or multiplied yield method is preferred where there are frequent significant changes in work-in-process (WIP) inventory at several operation steps, and where there are long throughput times from start to finish for the overall operation. When the operation has frequent significant changes in WIP inventory, just looking at parts into the first operation and comparing it to good parts out of the final operation gives a distorted measure of yield unless factored for the inventory changes, which might require some assumptions. Also, if the operation has long throughput times, say several weeks, and the production volume or mix is dynamic, volumes or mixes are likely to be dissimilar at the two ends of the operation, and again, merely comparing input parts to output parts would give a distorted measure of yield.

Where WIP inventories are generally stable, volumes and mixes not very dynamic, and throughput times relatively short, comparison of input and output numbers is appropriate, and, indeed, preferred. A frequent special case where this applies is in continuous process streams such as manufacture of window glass by the float process, where throughput times are measured in hours. Many other continuous process stream operations fall in this category. Often, so do one-step operations such as injection molding.

What we have discussed here is measuring the yield of an overall operation, and we have highlighted some of the weaknesses in those measures. However, none of those issues applies to calculating yields at an individual operation step; there, dividing the number of good parts out by the number of parts into the operation is generally straightforward. (There are some exceptions, however, such as when you have to fill up an empty continuous furnace at the beginning of a week or of a shift. In that case, you must note that output should not equal input.)

In some plants which make many products and are run like a job shop — that is, most items are only intermittently manufactured rather than being in continuous production — production reporting is done by manufacturing lot (or work order). This has the advantage of your being able to collect costs and performance by lot, so that when the job is completed, it is relatively easy to determine whether the job was profitable and by how much, and where the original estimates and expectations differed from what actually occurred.

It is often difficult, however, to learn and to improve an operation not in continuous production, and to catch problems early (because of the start and stop nature of the activity that makes changes in losses less noticeable.) Another subtle problem with this kind of reporting is that most measures of early (upstream) operation performance represent what was done some time ago, and do not provide a current snapshot of performance and results. Both the output divided by input and the cumulative yield methods of reporting usually show a current picture of performance at every process step, and are much more useful for tracking progress on process improvement.

Production reporting should always be broken down by production item. You should be able to identify the yields and all other major data for each item (stock keeping unit or SKU) manufactured.

Losses by Defect

Probably the most important information for problem solving and process improvement on a good production report is the breakdown of losses by defect. What that means is that all units not made into good parts at a particular operation step should be categorized by the defect for which they were rejected. At least all the major categories should be shown with the number of parts rejected for that defect at that operation. This information enables the process engineer to have available a ready-made Pareto diagram by loss for each step. Also, by checking the losses for recent days, the engineer can determine when or whether those individual defect losses trended up or down and perhaps associate the trend with an event. She may also observe the losses for that defect for the next days or weeks after taking corrective action to see if the action was effective.

Material Balance and Unaccounted

A quick way to test the adequacy of the production reporting system is to measure whether it provides a material balance, which explains what has happened to 99% of the material that entered the process. What has been lost (how many pieces and for which defects) at each operation step? How much material has been lost for volatilization? How much at each step for designed-in nonutilization (unused ends or borders or holes punched out, etc.)?

A rule of thumb for a good production report is that it should explain the outcome of 99% of the material entering the process. However, if you were making platinum objects or diamond jewelry, you would probably want at least one and probably two more decimal places of reporting detail because of the material value. Likewise, if you were processing sand and gravel, you might be content with 98% of entering material accounted for.

A related but somewhat different rule of thumb involves the maximum amount of allowed "unaccounted for" in a production report for discrete parts. Unaccounted usually is characterized by smaller amounts of product entering process steps than are shown as the "good pieces out" of the prior operation. Somewhere, you have lost track (but not reported as reject pieces) of product that was in the manufacturing queue. When this occurs systematically, you have reason to suspect the possibility of skullduggery or dishonesty. Someone may be deliberately refusing to acknowledge losses. The maximum amount of unaccounted expected in a good production report is 1%.

Downtime Reporting

You need to know about downtime to evaluate how much productive capacity was lost because of it, where problems are showing up, and how it is impacting operations. This information can often be used directly to justify the purchase of new equipment or the overhaul or upgrade of existing equipment.

The impact of downtime on an operation that has a long start-up time (perhaps to reach thermal equilibrium before good parts can be made) may be considerably more than the downtime itself. Often, downtime of a "simple" nature can cascade downstream, and prove to be much more costly than the "simple" cause might lead one to expect. This is especially true as plants adopt just-in-time practices that minimize or eliminate WIP buffers between operations. Whenever downtime is reported, you need to know what its cause is. It is the downtime causes that you can act upon. So, "downtime by cause" is another requirement for your model production report.

Rate and Other Required Data

Almost all readers of production reports are concerned with the rate at which product is being produced. We believe that equally important is the "SOP rate" that shows the speed the operation should be running at to perform best for the integrated requirements of quality and cost. In many operations, running too fast can result in poor quality or lower yields — thermal and chemical processes are obvious examples — so deviations from SOP rate need to be noted in both directions. Our suggestion is that actual rate and SOP rate should be provided on the report for each operation step for the period covered.

Generally, SOP rate will be "fixed" information that will only change from time to time, but it will usually be different for each item. We have noticed that it is useful information to include not only for the supervisor and analyst, but it is often used by operators to guide them during changeovers. It is therefore important to be careful that it is correctly stated on the report. Our observation is that telling operators that they should use the SOP, the fundamental information source, rather than production reports, works consistently only in those factories located in close proximity to heaven.

Detail in the production report can be broken down in many ways. The time dimension is often shown by day and shift showing parts in and good parts out as well as yield percentages. Showing week-to-date (typically the report of Monday's operations will show last week's percentages) is often quite helpful, as can be month-to-date and year-to-date when shown on weekly and monthly summary reports.

Often, supervisors and engineers, in their thirst for information, may ask for very fine breakdowns (by machine, line, operator, product variation, etc.) which can reduce the quantities in a particular box to such small numbers that what is observed and tracked is mostly noise. We urge that this be avoided. In startup processes, especially, it is a good idea to delay fine breakdowns until quantities are appropriate, and the principle applies as well to established processes. What you need to tell constituents is that production report data should be stable and meaningful enough to be a basis for action or understanding, and when it becomes primarily noise, it serves neither purpose. Furthermore, the many meaningless numbers on the production report tend to obscure the more significant information.

For the many operations where product movement into and out of WIP significantly affects the apparent yield numbers, the production report should show the WIP at the conclusion of the time slice reported, as well as the delta WIP, or change in WIP, at that point since the last report. With this information, analysts can reconcile and understand true yield and inventory status.

Often, the information we suggest including on the production report may be missing from the current version of the report, but is available in several other reports, perhaps issued by production control, quality control, inventory management, etc. We strongly urge that the information be integrated on this one report, perhaps simplifying or eliminating other current reporting. Ease of use and availability determine the degree to which information is scrutinized and put to use, and our observation is that having the necessary information all together results in much more effective action based on report numbers.

For complex operations where the report includes pages of detailed data, we suggest that the report be issued in segmented and hierarchical form. The most detail over a particular segment of the operation should be issued to those supervisors and managers deeply concerned with that area. Higher-level managers or other persons with broader scope should receive summary information covering the entire operation. A few trials should suffice to find the version that satisfies individual recipients.

Although it is quite possible to generate excellent production reports manually, as was done for generations, these days that is unnecessary and wastefully expensive. In another chapter, computerization of process discipline systems is discussed in more detail.

A sample production report that reflects many of the comments above is shown in Figure 9.1.

Figure 9.1 Production Report Example

OPERATION Shift/Product	Pieces In	Pieces Out	% Yield	% Standard	Cycle Rate (Pcs/Mach Hr)	% Possible	Downtime Hrs	Downtime Reason	A	B	C	D	E	F	G	H	I
1. RECEIVE BLANKS																	
DAY	75006	73616	98	111	3000	68			37	146	721	462					24
2. DRILL																	
MIDNITE -14	13652	13504	99	115	425	91	1.5	Hydraulic	17	56	3	19	41				12
-15	10673	10032	94	100	375	81		Leak	111	208	64	72	137				49
DAY -14	14007	13964	100	119	425	92			2	11	1	9					2
-15	10541	10061	95	101	375	82			30	211	5	43	189				
AFTN -14	13991	13327	95	113	425	90			171	251	32	38	167				
-15	10636	10482	99	105	375	86			12	91		1	50				5
3. ACID ETCH																	
MIDNITE -14	13521	13521	100	114	600	99	1	Prev Maint									
-15	10226	10226	100	106	600	100											
DAY -14	13610	13610	100	115	600	99											
-15	10290	10290	100	106	600	100											
AFTN -14	13692	13692	100	115	600	100											
-15	10060	10060	100	104	600	98											
4. PRESSURE TEST																	
MIDNITE -14	13472	13337	99	117	680	98			10	11	1	77	28				8
-15	10318	10220	99	115	680	99			1			67	30				
DAY -14	13702	13641	100	120	680	99			7	2		46	6				
-15	10111	10067	100	113	680	98			4	2		26	12				
AFTN -14	13641	13427	98	117	680	97			3	18		106	79				
-15	10146	9983	98	112	680	98			7	17	4	101	27				
5. PRINT																	
DAY -14	20152	19973	99	104	1200	81			2	18		37	26	89			7
-15	15097	14977	98	103	1200	82			6	14		22	14	48	16		
AFTN -14	20253	20109	99	105	1200	82				2				142			
-15	15173	14999	99	103	1200	82				18				156			

Figure 9.1 Production Report Example (cont.)

OPERATION Shift/Product	Pieces In	Pieces Out	% Yield	% Standard	Cycle Rate (Pcs/Mach Hr)	% Possible	Downtime Hrs	Downtime Reason	Losses by Defect								
									A	B	C	D	E	F	G	H	I
6. FIRE*																	
MIDNITE -14	14850	14553	98	108	525	91			114	66	86			29			
-15	11124	10880	98	117	600	91			132	8	69			35			
DAY -14	13612	13408	99	100	525	89			90	22	84				8		
-15	10264	9915	97	108	600	89			100	17	126			31	75		
AFTM -14	11620	11384	97	105	525	92			123		53			9	51		
-15	8588	8210	96	109	600	90			140		107			31	42		58
									A	B	C	D	E	F	G	H	I
7. INSPECT																	
DAY -14	39342	38702	98	148	1840	95			48	41	111	57	24	114	110	106	29
-15	29005	28335	98	114	1840	95			69	76	81	136	62	153	101	58	34

*OVERTIME UTILIZED

CUMULATIVE % YIELD:
Product 14 = 91%
Product 15 = 87%

DEFECT CODES

A. BROKEN
B. CRACKED
C. WARPED
D. OUT OF TOLERANCE ON LINEAR DIMENSIONS
E. HOLES OFF CENTER
F. RESOLUTION
G. INCOMPLETE
H. SPLOTCHES
I. MISCELLANEOUS OTHER

One of the authors visited a high-tech startup in Europe a few years ago, and found, amazingly, that the factory did not issue a production report. The production manager said that he did not see any reason to issue a report, since all the data were accessible on their computer network, and all key people were on the network. The production manager was asked how often the key people assembled to review the previous day's or week's data, and to discuss and plan action on the issues which the report highlighted. The answer was "never," because it was assumed that those directly responsible were reviewing the data and taking needed action individually. As the answer indicated, not only was there no production report, but there was also no production meeting. It was proposed to the production manager that he assemble his lieutenants daily to review and discuss printouts of the recent results, and make plans to respond to any indicated problems. He never did. The plant was unable to deliver working samples that met specification on their most important new product, and shut down not long afterward.

The most important thing about a production report is how thoroughly it is scrutinized, analyzed, and followed up with action. The worst report that is deeply studied and acted upon is far better than the ideal report which is largely ignored. The production report is a key element of the plant's most important feedback system, but how effectively you implement corrective action is the ultimate measure of its usefulness.

Strategic Maintenance Management

Why Is Maintenance Strategic?

Maintenance has major leverage on manufacturing performance. Let us consider some of the sources of company gain from excellent maintenance.

One group of benefits derives from downtime reduction, the avoidance of breakdowns, and their resultant work stoppages. These provide increased equipment and labor utilization, improved customer service, increased plant capacity, and reduced cumulative startup time.

Another group of benefits derives from improved equipment performance, which results in higher yields and better product quality, improved customer service, and stronger market position (because the plant can comfortably make the highest quality products whenever customers want them).

A third set of advantages comes from the efficiencies and cost reductions associated with well-managed activities. Reduced stockroom inventories and higher turns are coupled with improved stockroom service (higher percentage of having the needed item, being able to locate it, and have it be the correct revision for the replacement needed), reduced obsolescence, and shorter wait times and downtimes. This sounds like perpetual motion machine benefits, but this combination of results often happens when maintenance first becomes managed, and then well managed. Downtime reduction, improved equipment performance, and better inventory management lead to reduced maintenance overtime and reduced outside contracting.

A less obvious but quite likely benefit that goes along with excellent maintenance is longer equipment life. In capital intensive businesses, this is especially important.

Guidelines for Strategic Maintenance Management

A number of key things must be done on an ongoing basis to establish excellent maintenance. Most of them involve being well organized, keeping good records, doing thorough planning, and analyzing the data and taking appropriate action. However, these things are often counter-cultural to the "heroic" rescuer of the process from some emergency, the image that impelled many maintenance leaders into the profession.

While there is no doubt that equipment and services knowledge is necessary to the successful maintenance manager, it is equally important that the person have organizational and analytical skills, and the ability to identify generic problems early and take needed action in concert with production management. As will be seen, most of the guidelines refer to the management side of the job, an area where maintenance leaders are sometimes deficient. Here are the guidelines:

1. Establish an organization with supervisors and skilled specialists who are suited by experience and training for maintenance, and who have specialist knowledge and management/clerical skills. They must appreciate the need for operating in an organized mode, for collecting good data, and for making effective use of it. There should be an appropriate balance of skills for the plant situation, and adequate numbers of personnel.

2. Use a work order system that collects accurate data and forms the basis for equipment records, job planning, work scheduling, and manpower forecasting.

3. Develop downtime reporting. Number equipment and record running time. Reference downtime to running time for tracking and analysis. Keep equipment histories of production performance, and of maintenance actions and costs.

4. Analyze performance and cost. Measure and chart key indices. Take appropriate corrective action.

5. Make a weekly forecast. Schedule each week's work by the middle of the previous week. Prepare a daily schedule in advance to assure that maintenance personnel will not have to wait for assignments. Analyze and plan jobs in advance. Define required crafts, personnel, tools and materials, as well as the job to be done.

6. Establish a lubrication program and an equipment inspection program.

7. Train supervisors and maintenance personnel in management, technical skills, and process discipline.

8. Improve or replace equipment to eliminate chronic problems identified from the data.

9. Develop opportunity maintenance* to take advantage of unavoidable downtime, and modules of replacement** to speed and simplify getting equipment back up and running.

10. Provide continuously improving inventory control and storeroom management. Set up and meet targets of higher inventory turns and of lower frequency of outage of needed spares.

11. Work with engineering to maintain equipment drawings current, so the correct spare parts are inventoried. Keep all spare parts in defined locations, and have that information accessible.

Every plant that follows these guidelines will improve its operations — not just its maintenance. It takes a lot of work, but it is not rocket science. Use of the computer simplifies the work significantly. Following the guidelines enables the plant to take advantage of the leverage excellent maintenance can have on company performance.

The benefits of strategic maintenance management are usually significantly greater when operating under process discipline. Because the process is defined and documented and running in consistent fashion, operators are well trained, processes are audited, and introduction of change is controlled, the combination of these factors makes it much more likely that the full benefit of better equipment performance will be achieved. It is similarly more likely that these benefits will drop through to the bottom line, and not be masked or lost because of other process variabilities. The situation often provides both positive and negative motivation to the maintenance organization. Expectations are higher, and any-

---

*Opportunity maintenance — A program to take advantage of unscheduled downtime to accomplish other maintenance which can only be done when the line is down, or which can be done more easily at that time. The program requires establishing a "backlog" of maintenance actions "at the ready" with parts, materials, and detailed instructions.

**Modules of replacement — An operational policy of replacing assemblies or subassemblies intact, and troubleshooting and repairing them in the shop. This requires decisions about the level of assemblies to be replaced, and having spare assemblies available. The payoff is quicker, simpler fixes to get the line back up.

thing less than excellent equipment performance is visible and noticed and becomes the subject of complaint. On the other side, maintenance is not limited in access to the equipment, the equipment is operated properly, the process operates in a stable and successful mode, and both operations and maintenance usually enjoy the benefits.

Tooling Management

"Tooling" is a generic word with quite different meanings across a spectrum of industries. In some cases it refers to devices of extreme precision whose dimensions need to be measured by "fringes of light," and in others by relatively large fractions of an inch or centimeter. However, in almost all cases the accuracy of the tooling determines the best accuracy one can expect from the product. In some businesses, tools last indefinitely, but in most situations, they deteriorate with use and time. Without presenting a tooling management system per se, we will discuss those things most commonly included and controlled by those systems.

In a process discipline environment, you are deeply concerned with the management and control of tooling. An incorrect or obsolete (never updated to the latest change) tool can be the cause of manufacture of thousands of defective parts. Errors in CAD or CAM tooling software, or even in the designation of a revision, can likewise be responsible for production disasters. The control of change, the accuracy of tool drawings and tapes, and calibration of tool measuring instruments all must be as near-perfect as possible. You can think of tooling as some great magnifier that can make a great many good or bad units; you use process discipline to control the magnifier so it works only in beneficial ways.

Elements of Tooling Management

1. A current tool drawing should be available with drawing number, revision number, and latest date. If this is only available on CAD, all potential users must be trained to retrieve

the drawing. Since many companies carry several different revisions of a tool (to make different revisions of the part), it is essential that revisions and any other particularization (LH, upper, outboard, etc.) be specifically identified. If the tool shape is identified electronically, revisions and the other particulars should be carried through to tool paths, tapes, etc.

2. The storage location of the tool should be indicated, wherever possible located to the specific unambiguous spot on the shelf or floor.

3. Where appropriate, any storage environment requirements should be specified, as should any protective coatings, lubrication, etc.

4. A tool readiness document should indicate what dimensions must be established or checked on the tool before it can be used in production. Every requirement the toolmaker must guarantee should be shown.

5. A tag or other appropriate paperwork should move with the tool showing the signature and date of the toolmaker who has checked out the tool prior to this use. It is often helpful for the tag to show several of the previous guarantors and the dates of their work.

6. If intermediate maintenance of the tool is required between uses, the tool readiness document should indicate that, and another tag for that work should also be with the tool with appropriate signoffs.

7. When the tool is removed after being run, it should be checked and signed off by a toolmaker who specifies that it seems visually OK for reuse.

It is important to assign a serial number (and inscribe it if possible) for each tool, and to maintain a historical data base that includes at least the following for each time the tool is run:

■ tool name, drawing number, serial number, storage location;

■ toolmaker who prepared it for this run,

- quantity of rejects by defect during this run,

- number of parts processed, total number of defects, overall yield;

- hours, minutes run, average rate, why the tool was removed or the run stopped;

- dimensional performance for key dimensions for this run such as mean or median dimensions, histograms or ranges for those dimensions, etc.;

- how performance on this run compared to historical data for (1) this tool and (2) for all similar tools as a class. Often, this can be done by showing YTD (year to date) numbers.

The tooling database should use data provided by process discipline reporting systems (e.g., the production report, maintenance reports, quality reports), perhaps requiring some changes in these to meet its specific requirements. But tooling data, maintenance data, production data, and quality data should come from the same reliable source(s) so they are never in conflict.

How elaborate the database should be is a function of the sensitivity of the process to the tooling quality, and this varies from operation to operation. The most important requirement for a database of this kind is that it be reviewed and analyzed systematically. Depending on frequency of tool use, the data should be analyzed, a report published, and a management review meeting for decision-making held at least annually, and perhaps as often as quarterly.

Related Technologies and Activities

This book focuses on process discipline; however, it impinges on and makes use of many related technologies and activities which should be integrated with process discipline for a manufacturing business to be most effective. Some of these include:

- calibration
- materials management

- new product development

- quality control

- statistical process control

- ISO 9000/QS-9000/GMP/HACCP

Each of those has been the subject of many books, and detailed discussions of them cannot be included here. However, there are some issues to be noted with respect to process discipline, and some key references supplied on these topics.

Calibration

We espouse data-based decision-making as a fundamental pillar of process discipline. The data come from measuring instruments, and can never be better than the state of calibration of those devices. Similarly, the decisions can never be better than the data. So, in a rational organization, decision quality is directly related to the effectiveness of the calibration program.

The more sophisticated the product, the more likely it is that its performance, and often its acceptability, depend on elaborate or highly precise measurements and settings made during its manufacture. The profitability of the firm and the goodness of its products — two of the most important determinants of its success and survival — thus rely on the accuracy of its measurements. The calibration system has been devised to assure that instruments are operating at close to their utmost capability so that those measurements are consistently good — basic process discipline. Most manufacturing businesses must have effective calibration systems to protect their bottom-line economics, their products' reputation, and to operate with the full benefits of process discipline.

Commercial software packages are now available to do the record keeping, to trigger actions required during the current period, and to highlight special problems. These can run on personal computers, offer graphic outputs, and eliminate the drudgery. They also provide excellent support for QS and ISO system needs.

The question is frequently raised about whether it is necessary to include in the calibration program instrumentation which is an integral part of production equipment — such as the controllers on a furnace — because those devices are not used to make ultimate decisions about the product. Often the sheer volume of calibration effort motivates their omission from the program. In our view, that is a mistake. While problems in these instruments may not directly affect the quality of product to the customer, they do have a direct impact on yields, cost, and customer service. Furthermore, omission violates the principle of process discipline to assure prevention. And, as a practical matter, when problems of this sort occur, they are often very expensive.

Calibration is difficult to start in a factory because it requires an investment in measuring standards and sometimes in better instruments, it requires dedicated good quality space — temperature and often humidity controlled — and the assignment of trained and knowledgeable personnel. There is a front-end financial load, but calibration becomes a silent bulwark assuring the quality of your measurements and providing true management by prevention. The key requirement with calibration is to be sure that everyone abides by the rules. Never use an instrument with an outdated calibration sticker, and never pass up a required recalibration.

Materials Management

Materials management offers opportunities for improvement through adoption of process discipline systems both externally and internally. The use of process discipline externally means, in simplest terms, getting your suppliers to implement the same process discipline systems as you yourself have implemented. You would like to think of your suppliers (and they would generally like to be thought of) as a backward extension of your production lines, with the same reliability and level of control (at least) as your own operations. Suppose you have done a good job of using the manufacturing systems to reduce variability in order to bring the process into statistical control. Be sure you have implemented information and audit programs that provide fast feedback loops. That way you will learn early enough when things may be heading out of control so that you can still take action to prevent or minimize the adverse effects. Obviously, if your supplier has not progressed equally down this route, you are likely to be disappointed in his performance. Your expectations have been raised by the improvement in your own performance as you learned to put these systems to work; unless the vendors are performing to your new level, you will suffer because of their weakness. Materials management must assure that suppliers are taught the same methods used internally, and that they get the same results.

Internally, within the materials management function, you have to eliminate errors and develop systems that are as nearly fail-safe as possible. You should enforce change control as effectively in procurement as you do in manufacturing. Proof that changes are accomplished, are effective, and do not incur adverse consequences needs to be demonstrated before changes are approved.

Another important issue when dealing with suppliers is the exact delineation of how a change will be implemented — which lines, which specific SKUs, which plants will change when, and which items or plants will remain the same. Purchasing departments also need to understand that if several vendors' materials all meet specification, that does not mean they are all alike, or can be freely substituted for each other without process consequences. Process discipline usually requires much more precision in planning and communication on the part of materials management to avoid errors or erroneous assumptions on the part of any of the players.

New Product Development

As new products and processes are developed, if you want successful, timely manufacturing startup and product introduction, the fundamental elements of process discipline must be completed and fully ready for use when the first transition to pilot manufacture commences. This means documents completed, people trained to the documents, audits designed with forms available and people trained to use them, change control established and the entire organization taught the rules and procedures, and an experiment planning system in place. This is a necessary price of a successful startup, and it has been proven repeatedly.

Here is a list of comments that will virtually guarantee bad startups and transitions:

1. We do not know enough yet to write the documents. We will provide temporary brief lists of sequential steps and of trial settings.

2. We do not yet know how to audit this process because we are still trying to learn the correct way ourselves.

3. The people will be trained by our development experts sitting at their side (called Next-to-Nellie in the United Kingdom because of the implied proximity of trainer and trainee) because we do not have time to write it all down, and our people learn by doing, not from paper.

4. We have to make lots of changes because we are still learning and experimenting in this early phase, so it is necessary for us to be more informal about changes in order to keep up with the pace of process evolution. When the process stabilizes, we will move to formal change control.

5. Our people are doing a good job of "private" experimenting on their process steps, and they tell us about the successful ones so we can include the new methods in the process.

If you hear one of these comments, protest immediately. If you hear more than two, ask to be reassigned to another project.

Quality Control

Quality control is still a valid set of mathematically based practices. Every organization needs to have incoming inspection (performed in-house or by the vendor), in-process checks which are usually done by SPC, and final inspection to provide data which support that the product meets specification to designated quality levels. By now, everyone knows that quality cannot be inspected in; it must be built in by operation with controlled processes. The more stringent the quality requirements, the more overwhelmingly true this statement is.

The practices detailed in this book were developed and implemented to achieve the utmost in manufacture of high quality products. They were originally used to meet six ppm (parts per million maximum defective) requirements decades ago, and have since been applied many times to attain similarly tight requirements. Process discipline works in tandem with sampling, SPC, statistically designed experiments, and other traditional quality control techniques from limit samples to computerized contour measurement. Statistics and quality control, just as they have always been, are necessary for you to keep score, to protect your customers, and to make sure that what you are currently producing will become good salable product. Process discipline provides increased dimensions of variability reduction, and of preservation and "lock-in" of learning. With the use of process discipline, the rate of improvement is speeded and the final quality levels are raised well beyond what was previously attainable. But, quality control is still an essential element in the toolbox.

Statistical Process Control

Everything anyone needs to know about SPC was beautifully captured and described in the Western Electric Statistical Quality Control Handbook first printed in 1956, probably the best technical publication ever issued by a commercial organization. Neither Western Electric nor their parent company, AT&T, exist in their original form today, but you must hope that this volume will continue to be available for many years to come. This book is so good that much of the material can be learned by an intelligent amateur in one careful reading. The use of simple graphics for diagnosis and trouble-shooting throughout the book is especially outstanding.

The handbook covers much more than SPC, but the material on SPC (invented at Western Electric) is the first and last word on the subject. Since SPC is now an acknowledged basic technology that should be used by all, every plant and technical organization ought to have a copy. No one else needs to write about SPC (and we will not either), except perhaps to note that software is now widely available to do the calculations and the graphing.

SPC charts (or Shewhart charts, after the inventor) are an excellent tool for learning about the process, for trouble-shooting, for identifying causes, and for determining if fixes really work. When it was originally developed, SPC was touted as a great method for maintaining processes in control. These days, other automatic feedback systems usually respond faster and are more effective at long-term control, but SPC provides many benefits. Using SPC and following its guidelines, you know when to leave the process alone; that is, when *not* to make a move because there is no significant indication of an out-of-control situation. SPC is really the only system which tells you that, and some electronic control systems have now incorporated SPC decision-making into their controllers to limit their action to situations which demand it. Imitation is the sincerest form of flattery.

SPC charts also show us how good a job is being done at running the process centrally on the nominal. This may seem to contradict the previous point about not responding except to out-of-control indications, but the difference is between the short term and the long term. In the short term, you want to only move in situations that *require* action. But, in the long term, you want to be centered on the allowed operating range. This is often an issue of precision setup.

It has always been beneficial to run at the center; Taguchi expressed this with his quadratic loss function that identifies a cost proportional to the square of the distance from the center of the allowed range. It has become even more important in recent years when customers are increasingly specifying cpk's for critical dimensions. Cpk is a ratio which relates the distributional spread (from the standard deviation), the allowed tolerance range, and how centrally the distribution fits in the tolerance range (oversimplified, it is how many spreads will fit in the tolerance range).

The more central, the higher the cpk, which puts the supplier in the most favorable position. By making use of SPC visuals, firms can determine how effective they are, and they can often impute what action is necessary to improve. SPC is another example of a technology that complements process discipline, and SPC is particularly helpful in solving assignable cause problems in column two of the flow chart.

ISO 9000/QS-9000/GMP/HACCP

The letter scramble above represents, of course, a variety of the international and domestic quality and related system standards that most commercial (and other) organizations find themselves subject to by law or by commercial reality. ISO 9000 is the international quality system standard, QS-9000 is the almost identical U.S. auto industry system, GMP stands for the FDA's Good Manufacturing Practices, and HACCP is the Hazard Analysis and Critical Control Point program, also primarily aimed at pharmaceutical and food companies. All of these have been developed to bring more control to manufacture and other processing, and there are similarities and overlaps among these.

Process discipline was developed to make manufacturing superb — top quality, high yield, low cost, predictable customer service, and boring consistency. It was not initiated to qualify for or to "pass" any national or international standard. However, our experience has been that plants with good existing process discipline have always had a very easy time qualifying. Almost everything needed was already in place, and generally operating under more stringent rules than required by the standards bodies.

We have learned, though, that prior qualification to those standards does not necessarily imply strong systems that guarantee good quality or consistent manufacturing. The reason seems to be that one can satisfy the requirements doing all the minimums, and without requiring proof, statistical significance, and the other rigors that provide the real discipline. Process discipline is more demanding, but it delivers. It is worth it if your goal is superb manufacturing.

CHAPTER 10

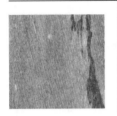

CULTURAL ISSUES

Inertia and Other Forms of Resistance

In any manufacturing facility the amount of work to be done always and inevitably outstrips the amount of resources available to do it. If this were not the case, there would be far fewer headache remedies on the market, and far less stress at monthly production reviews.

When someone comes along with notions of how to improve your lot in life by making your processes more consistent, they are contending with many other ideas as to how best to use your time and resources. "It's a great idea," you will tell them. "Good luck in implementing it (in some other department)."

It is the busiest factories — the ones most likely to realize immediate gains from the work of process discipline — which are least likely to want to begin the journey. They resist packing their bags, let alone calling the cab that will take them to the airport. So how can you overcome this inertia? What causes some factories to adapt easily to the process discipline environment, embrace the work that needs to be done, and reap the benefits, while others languish in the status quo?

In the dozens of plants where we have successfully led efforts to bring about process discipline, there is always a champion of the ideas embodied in process discipline. At least one person in the factory — because of intellectual bent, because of prior experience in another environment, or perhaps from benchmarking exceptionally prosperous enterprises elsewhere — provides the necessary leadership to make things happen. This person is not necessarily at the top of the chain of command, and is not likely to be at the bottom either. It might be a department head or an engineering manager. It might be the operations manager or the controller. Somewhere in the factory there must be someone who understands and embraces the philosophy of process discipline and who has the perseverance to see it through. This champion must be willing to quell the riots and lead the charge, to calm the dissidents and negotiate with terrorists. Without at least one champion, there is little hope of causing the changes that must occur.

It is our intention that those who are reading this book are examining our logic and testing our premises against what they know about their own operations. We intend to create champions of process discipline. And it is our fervent hope that those champions will begin the work that must be done to create an environment of process discipline.

In the beginning there will be many reasons why now is not a good time. It is the first objective of the champion(s) to overcome such inertia by making some small and realistic inroad that can then open other channels. A good choice is a process that engineers and production supervisors are confident can be cured with process consistency.

You should ensure that those whose names are most prominently associated with early efforts in process discipline have the high regard and wide respect of your organization's leadership. If this is not the case — especially in the beginning—then much of your energy will be diverted.

While one might safely predict where certain quarters of resistance will be found, there is an unexpected and subtle pocket which tends to be well camouflaged. Many manufacturing organizations have long rewarded a particular kind of behavior that ostensibly is geared toward problem solving. The heroes and heroines of such an organization are anointed for their quick and responsive handling of whatever problems are tossed their way. Without process discipline, the problems come at a dizzying pace—and so do the exceptional contribution or above-and-beyond or whatever other awards are handed out to those who are best at fighting fires. Most of these people do not consciously want to foment problems, yet the prevailing reward system can cause them to resent efforts to create a more stable environment. The best tactic here is to enlist them early in your efforts and ensure that there are appropriate incentives for creating, supporting, and maintaining process consistency for problem prevention. Make sure that the old reward system is carefully analyzed and realigned so that heroism is identified as the perpetuation of process discipline.

The forces perpetuating the status quo are typically opposed to something as inclusive as process discipline. When it is integrated well, there are few members of the organization who are not influenced by its new rigor and requirements. It is necessary, then, to understand who has a stake in preserving the way things are today and to create some value for them in attaining the results you want to achieve. Sometimes this can be done by reviewing and changing the objectives set for them. In extreme cases, it is necessary to move them to non-influential slots where they cannot impede the work you plan to do. Since their potential for diluting your efforts and diverting your attention is plain, you must identify and address these issues before you begin.

Gaining Acceptance and Embedding the Culture

Gaining Acceptance

So much good comes from process discipline that acceptance usually follows fairly quickly once people begin to see the results.

Early detractors, however, often look for opportunities to reinforce their original cynicism; and, if they can, they will try to attribute positive results to other causes. Since in most factories it is common to have overlapping initiatives to bring about improvements, clear attribution to process discipline alone is sometimes difficult. For this reason (and because it makes good business sense anyway), it is a good idea to clearly define the *before* status of the pilot area. If you have selected the pilot area based on the potential for early success, then there are likely to be real measures of the problems which you expect to be solved (or at least considerably ameliorated) by the addition of process discipline. Production statistics can usually be used to supply the data. Post-acquired data, even when they are scrupulously taken from historic records, are often suspected (by an already skeptical group of people) of being selectively chosen. Our advice is to agree before implementation that process discipline ought to cause improvement in some set of statistics, then measure both before and after.

Choosing the appropriate statistics need not be difficult. If you ran this process to the very best of your ability, what do you imagine would be different from the way things are today? Scrap and rework are two obvious measures you would expect to improve. Customer complaints (where they relate directly to controllable cosmetic or functional defects in the product) are another. Any of the many textbooks on TQM include suggestions for other candidates for measures of success since the cost of quality includes those things you do over because they were not done correctly the first time.

When data show the positive results that follow process discipline, we recommend that they be recorded, broadly publicized, and retained for historical reasons.

In newer or more enlightened operations, there can be an early consensus that process discipline provides the necessary conditions for operational success. In such situations, the temptation is to forego any documentation or data about the "betterness" of things. We caution you only that, at some point in the predictable future, the easy conviction that the effect was well worth the effort is destined to come into question. It is prudent, then, to acknowledge in some public forum the role process discipline has played in a successful ramp-up or a smooth transfer of technology or whatever the case may be.

Embedding the Culture

Early success can cause runaway enthusiasm and a strong desire to quickly replicate results across the entire organization. This, too, can be a danger. Since you fully expect process discipline to become a way of life, you ought to ensure that the foundation you lay will withstand the sometimes-withering assaults of day-to-day life in a production facility. Resist the temptation to declare victory too early in the game. We have listed here some of the underpinnings which will ensure that process discipline takes root strongly and successfully.

Train new personnel as part of a core curriculum administered during the first few weeks post-hire. Training in this sense is separate from the training that occurs to impart job knowledge. We are talking here about a new-hire orientation that discusses the way you operate your processes in an overarching climate of process discipline. Plants we have worked with have developed both formal and informal ways of ensuring that respect for the rules of process discipline is conveyed early in each new employee's career. You can decide what works best for your organization. Videos, self-guided interactive computer programs, formal classroom training, booklets and brochures have all worked at one location or another.

While audits serve as the feedback monitor on the overall health of process discipline, they also are an important means of embedding the culture. They help instill an expectation of compliance and a format for routine discussion of problems that arise in maintaining the culture.

Once the groundwork has been laid and there has been substantial progress, here are some additional suggestions for ensuring that this new culture remains entrenched:

Make certain that your best people are closely associated with the program. Discuss the need for process discipline openly and often. When process upsets do occur, use process discipline as a format for trouble-shooting. If your operation routinely conducts personnel performance evaluations, include support of the process discipline philosophy as a key item for review. Periodically report on success stories — new equipment brought on line under process discipline, successful introduction of new products, customer feedback on the reduction of errors, etc. If you have a newsletter, construct a column specifically dedicated to anecdotes demonstrating how process discipline is working. Celebrate success on a regular basis.

Plants typically record the number of days since the last lost-time accident, using this as a key indicator that what you are doing for safety is working. It is similarly important to trumpet the *absence* of problems as a result of process discipline.

Finally, make certain that your annual operating plan contains specific process discipline objectives for each department. Include system enhancements (perhaps the addition of electronic technology), new training tools, and other proactive initiatives to keep the focus clear.

Recognizing Recidivism

After you have worked so hard to establish process discipline and have begun to prosper from the rewards it induces, your efforts turn to other endeavors. You have new products to design, customer issues to resolve, and bold new initiatives to undertake in your pursuit of excellence. This diversion of your attention can have unexpected repercussions for process discipline.

We have worked with many plants who were early adopters of the process discipline philosophy and who sought our assistance and support to re-establish some of the elements of process discipline that had drifted from their initial health. Sometimes we referred to these as back-to-basics campaigns. Often it was only a matter of a few weeks before the patient recovered. Occasionally it has been necessary to temporarily provide resources in order to get back on track. From time to time we have put in place whole teams of engineers and technicians.

Why does this happen in even the most dedicated of organizations? Is it inevitable, or is there something can do to prevent it from happening? You can expect that there will be some straying from time to time, particularly when there is a change in management. Audits are the feedback loop you use to signal that you are drifting away from process discipline, and their results *always* must be taken seriously in light of their important function in this regard.

CHAPTER 11

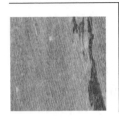

SUCCESSFUL
IMPLEMENTATION

Identifying Your Own Best Practices

When we first talk with a plant or a company regarding process discipline, there is usually a point in the discussion where we are asked the question, "Where do we begin?" The answer we give depends upon what is already in place. So the first step we recommend is a sort of self-analysis undertaken in order to identify your own best practices.

Most operations are doing a remarkably good job in many, many aspects of manufacturing management. In fact, strong elements of process discipline usually exist in even modestly successful operations. You usually find some form of documentation already in existence when you first start our work. Canvassing the production areas, you find logbooks and taped instructions and old memos at the workstations. You find some people have personal notebooks they carry to and from work on a daily basis, and they keep this information current and correct as they observe new facts about the process.

Quality assurance departments are veritable goldmines of process information, and much of it is accurate. Formal audits or "studies" may punctuate the calendar year and file cabinets are replete with the results. Engineering notebooks, if they are available, can contain mother lodes of carefully documented experiments and their results. The human resources department sometimes produces training materials that are rich in both current and historic process information.

So…what does your factory do well? How do people learn to do their jobs? Who do you turn to when process problem solving is required? How do you explain your process to visiting vendors or customers? What do you do when a piece of equipment fails? The answers to these questions and others you might think of will guide you in identifying your own best practices.

Perhaps you have an outstanding maintenance program that incorporates preventive maintenance as well as quick-change modules of replacement. Maybe your strength is in an outstanding calibration program or the training of inspection personnel. Has your new information systems manager set up a production information system that supports graphic analyses and SPC?

You can use the table of contents from this book to create a checklist for evaluating your current practices, and you should do this before you begin to make any changes in support of process discipline. Record what you do now under each of the subheadings. Be sure to include everything, even if what is being done is being done in only one department or is less than perfect in its execution. You will probably want to solicit input from department managers and support staff.

When you have completed the inventory of your current practices, use a high-medium-low or five-point scale to rank them. Since this is a qualitative exercise, opinions may vary. You should, however, end up with a list of "best practices" which can serve as the foundation of your new initiatives.

Building on your own best practices is important. If you do not take advantage of what people in your operations know to be good and useful, the credibility of your work to establish process discipline will be seriously undermined. In addition, using familiar source material increases acceptance and gives you a leg up on getting started.

The Optimal Sequence of Implementation

We find four basic situations when we start to work with a factory that has no prior history of a coherent and successful process discipline effort:

- Greenfield sites are too new to have developed much infra-structure at all, and they must start from scratch.

- Some plants are in the process of introducing major new processes or product lines and are planning to implement process discipline concurrent with the new technology.

- Some plants have very good antecedent systems that require fine-tuning and the addition of certain missing elements.

- Most operations have bits and pieces of good systems already in existence, and substantial process histories.

In spite of the seemingly dissimilar conditions in these situations, there is an implementation approach that will work in any of them. Someone will self-nominate or be appointed as the champion or project manager of implementation. Let us assume that you are that person.

When you have a clear idea in your own mind about how the elements of process discipline interact, the dynamics of implementation are clearer. The first requirement is some decision-making about what you want to have happen. You must decide whether you will tackle the entire operation or some subset of the operation, perhaps a certain department or a certain process area. If you decide that you will start with something less than the entire operation, then you must think about the implications for interdependent operations.

Let us suppose, for example, that you are the department head of a finishing operation for a large plant, and that your factory accords a great deal of autonomy to each department head.

You decide to champion process discipline, and you want to lead efforts by demonstrating success within your own operation. You will need to enlist the support of the engineers who work on processes and equipment within your department; and, of course, you will want to work closely with your team leaders and key operating personnel as well. You can document your processes and institute training, change control, audits, and experiment planning. If, however, you have not taken into consideration the broader needs of the factory in establishing your pilot system, you will probably find that other department heads have their own ideas about some of the ground rules that you have put in place. You can avoid having to undo or redo work by being inclusive in your early decision-making.

Let us suppose you are the staff-level project manager responsible for installing a new automated manufacturing line in a large facility known to have serious labor-relations difficulties. You can provide documentation and training for the new line, conduct careful experiments to ensure that the equipment and process produce acceptable product, and record all changes you make during the transition from staff to plant control. If you do all those things, your project will likely be successful — perhaps even ahead of schedule and within budget. We would not expect, however, that a visitor to the new installation after eight or nine months of operation would find that the documents are still current and the change control process is continuing without emphasis and support from local management.

As with any project of significant size, you will need to define the overall scope and then describe the phases of implementation. It is not always straightforward, and it will usually happen both serially and concurrently. Serially, in the sense that documents are written over some period, and can be scheduled for completion by process, by department, or by type. Concurrently, because the various elements can be brought on-stream at the same time, assuming you have done your homework.

Start with documentation. We say this because documents serve as the referent for training, for change control, and for audits.

However, you need not finish all documents before you begin to train. In fact, it is preferable to train to each document as it is completed. As soon as the training has been accomplished, any changes to the document must be made using change control. Audits can be conducted, then, to ensure that the trained workforce is running the process according to the documented procedure.

Someone must be responsible for organizing and coordinating the entire effort. This person need not be the champion of the process discipline philosophy. It might be preferable in your own operation to consider a small implementation team, under the mentorship of the champion. You will know best what it will take to ensure successful implementation.

Whether it is a single person or a small team, the first order of business will be to organize the program plan. The flow charts and flow sheets will determine what documents must be written, and then the writing schedule can be prioritized and authorship assigned.

There are reporting mechanisms which must be established, and decisions made about who will approve the documents and changes, who will be responsible for ensuring experiment plans are properly laid out, and how the plant will respond to audit discrepancies. Specific advice regarding the various elements that must be established can be found throughout the book, particularly in the chapters covering the fundamental elements of process discipline.

Common sense will guide you in much of the organizational decision-making that must take place. Your operation's ability to absorb these new tasks and to incorporate the changes required will dictate the timeline you set.

Communication During the Implementation Process

Whenever substantial change is taking place, people naturally speculate about what is going on and how it will affect them. Some people will assume that things are going to get better; others will take an opposite view; still others sit on the fence. One thing is certain, though, and that is that there will be communication taking place.

We are not aware of any program that has failed simply because of lack of communication. What does happen, though, is that miscommunication or absence of information diverts energy and dilutes focus. That is why we strongly recommend that you err on the side of overcommunication.

You will want to inform the plant about your intentions, what you believe will be required to make process discipline successful, and the outcome you expect. As with all other important undertakings, your success will be closely linked to your ability to enlist the support and cooperation of those who will be affected. While certain charismatic leaders can count on support from their followers even in the absence of information about what it is they are supporting, the rest of us must rely on information, logic, and persuasion to accomplish the task.

Here are some suggestions for such communication which have served others well:

- If you have a plant or company newsletter, submit a column for each issue that outlines the plans you have and the successes you have experienced to date. Solicit comments and contributions from those who have been affected by the work done to date.

- Conduct a monthly project review and issue an open invitation. Consider a brown bag lunch session so that those who cannot normally attend can participate.

- Take advantage of the corporate Web page, if you have one. Add a link and make your input visually exciting, perhaps focusing on the people that are making things happen in support of process discipline.

- Put up a bulletin board in a main hallway and post examples, pictures, comments, and other "news" so that people see the progress you are making.

- Set up a special e-mail site and encourage people to submit questions and comments. Be certain, though, if you do this that you respond thoroughly and in a timely manner.

If you are responsible for implementing process discipline and you are not particularly good at communication, consider assigning someone else to fill this important role. If you have ever participated in a training class led by someone whom you knew to be the most knowledgeable in the subject at hand, but whose communication skills were limited to reading the text aloud or mumbling jargon while facing the projection screen, you will have some idea of what is to be avoided.

In the hundreds of times we have presented our message of consistent operations to shop floor operators, we have always and unfailingly found that the vast majority of our audience eagerly embraces the concept of consistency. They tell us they strongly prefer to work under conditions of stability and consistency, and they confirm over and over that they understand the derivative benefits and are willing to do what is necessary to bring about the new environment of process discipline. This is true even in factories where management predicts that transmitting the message to production personnel will be chief among the obstacles we face in implementation.

When we say the "vast majority" is supportive, we mean exactly that. Every operation has a few renegades at all levels of personnel, and the shop floor almost always has one or more anarchists among the others. While guffaws and giggles often greet their vocal opposition to what we say, people call us aside after our presentation and tell us that their colleagues and teammates know these people to be detrimental to a healthy work environment. They further tell us they hope our program will cause some change in these people or that management will see fit to remove them from the workplace. Our own observation is that the most vocal opponents can become your most powerful allies if they are given the opportunity to participate in writing documents, auditing the process, or otherwise supporting the work that needs to be accomplished. If the reason that these people have become cynical and hostile is that they have heretofore been denied an active role in influencing their daily work, we suggest that you can use the introduction of process discipline as a tool to re-engage their commitment and energy.

In one medium-sized factory making traditional products, we had had some difficulty in getting process discipline off the ground. This factory was one of several that were under a corporate dictate to implement process discipline as a strategic initiative, but progress was being impeded by lack of support at the department head level. The head of the finishing department was an especially vocal opponent who felt strongly that there were better uses for the time we were requesting of him and of the people in his department. In a meeting with plant management to discuss how best to proceed with the implementation, one of the authors suggested that it would be a good idea if this particular department head would attend a multiplant training workshop in the hows and whys of process discipline which was held at corporate headquarters each fiscal quarter. We even agreed to forego the normal training fees if he returned to the plant still antagonistic toward the implementation schedule. After the three-and-a-half day workshop (attended by two dozen or so other participants from different plants), this formerly adverse individual returned home, set up an appointment with the plant manager, and asked to be assigned as project leader for process discipline implementation. He did a terrific job of ensuring that the implementation was successful and later returned to his department head position. He remained one of our staunchest supporters throughout the rest of his career.

Another common refrain when we begin to inform a factory workforce of the impending changes that process discipline will bring about is this: "We support the work you are doing, and we agree that it will help our plant. However, we certainly hope you intend to tell our engineers and team leaders and managers that they, too, will have to follow the rules." Let us acknowledge here that engineering and production, management and shop floor personnel are often at cross-purposes. There is often active disagreement as to how to run the process for the good of the product and the plant. This is troublesome ground, since the motives of all parties are generally benign. Fortunately, however, process discipline offers the help that is needed to sort things out. When a factory runs under strong process discipline, purposes are aligned and the infrastructure permits opposing factions to carry out their work under strong and meaningful ground rules.

Engineers are not allowed to "tinker" with the process without planned experiments. Operators are not allowed to "adjust" the process outside of the defined limits described in documents. Both engineers and operators must use the formal change control process to incorporate new information or revise information already documented.

Communication, therefore, implies that everyone in the factory hears the same message. That message must be as pervasive and consistent as the environment you want to create.

In one classroom where we were once observers, there was a very strong case being made for following documented safe work practices. About 20 minutes of the hour-long training was devoted to showing a film intended to reinforce safe workplace behavior. During the course of the film, a supervisor comes down an aisle and observed a worker at a machine that clearly had the safety shield moved aside. The supervisor stopped, the worker looked up sheepishly, and then he put the shield back into place. "I know I should have the guard down when I'm working, Bill," said the worker, "but I can't see the quality of the weld well enough to ensure I'll make a good part." Bill nodded in apparent agreement that he recognized the situation to be valid. "Well, safety first, Gerry. Keep that guard in place." He continued walking toward the office area, and one more worker has been placed in a quandary of management's making: Should he lift the guard and ensure the quality of his work? Or should he keep the guard down, knowing that he is risking a poorly made part? And what has the supervisor communicated about the decision he should make as to how to do his work? We can imagine that the next person to come down the same aisle is the quality assurance manager. She will pick up a part headed for a downstream operation, examine it, and ask Gerry why his work is of such poor workmanship.

We think the better answer is to talk about how to temporarily change the process so that Gerry can work safely *and* build good product until a permanent fix can be tested and implemented.

Another real-life example occurred some years ago in Louisville when a zealous supervisor was using newly created documents to train his shift workers in the right way to run the process. He read from the document: "Pick up the parts from the cart and remove the accompanying tag to identify the number...." A hand shot up. "But the tags sometimes are not attached," one of the participants stated with obvious frustration, "and so we cannot fill out the paperwork properly." The supervisor in his role as trainer continued, "Yes, but the document says to take the tag and...." Again a hand shot up. "We told you there aren't any tags." The instructor insisted that all questions and comments be held until he was finished with his "training." Anyone can imagine that the communication taking place was unilateral and destined to undermine the message the trainer was attempting to convey. We cannot follow documents that are not correct in their description of the process and do not provide for the real-life situations that will be encountered.

In both of the examples above, we are not challenging the intentions of the trainers, the quality of the equipment being used, nor the method of instruction. What we are taking to task here is the content of the message. We encourage you to think carefully about what you are communicating by your actions as well as your words. If you are serious about process discipline you must *yourself* be disciplined in the example you set and the message you deliver. The documents must *accurately* reflect the process. Not even the plant manager can change the process without using a change control form. The chief engineer cannot implement a change without backing it up with data from a valid experiment. The department manager must follow the document as surely as the off-shift worker must. Discrepancies discovered during the audit process must be followed up with true corrective action.

You communicate by your actions as well as by your words.

Measuring the Results

Throughout this book we have given examples and anecdotes of problems encountered and resolved through the application of process discipline and its principles. In many cases we have been able to assign specific numbers to validate the improvement we know to have occurred. Frequently, however, we cannot pinpoint the dollar value of the gains we have realized, although we are certain of them.

Inevitably you will be called upon, as a champion of process discipline, to prove that the resources expended have resulted in measurable benefits. We do not envy you the task since almost any "proof" you offer may be challenged by those who drag their heels on process discipline (usually because it requires work and discipline). Thus, it is necessary to introduce rigor into the process of measuring, so the savings become more difficult to refute.

In other sections of this book we have suggested that you should determine in advance of implementation some of the measures which you will use. It is important to know the "before" so that you can take stock of the "after" and derive the difference between the two conditions. Let us consider several different groups of metrics:

Group A

- Overall Yield (First Time Through)   By Product or Product Line
- Good Parts to Stock per Person   By Product or Product Line
- $ Value Receipted (or Shipped) per Person   By Product or Product Line
- Variable Cost per Unit (Normalized)   By Product or Product Line

Group B

■ Downtime as a % of Scheduled Hours	By Product Line
■ Median Throughput Time	By Product or Product Line
■ Rework Hours per Hundred Units Produced	By Product or Product Line
■ Scrap $ per Hundred Units	By Product or Product Line
■ Customer Complaints	By Product Line
■ $ Returns, Allowances, or Warranty Costs	By Product Line
■ % Delivery Promises Missed	By Product or Product Line

Group C

■ % Yield at Final Inspection	By Product or Product Line
■ PPM Quality at Customer for Critical/Major Defects	By Product or Product Line
■ % Accepted at Lot Sampling	By Product or Product Line
■ % Material Utilization — Overall Process	By Product Line
■ Market Share	By Product Line

It is useful to pick at least three of these from each group and track them weekly or monthly (whichever is most usually measured in your plant), showing the results graphically. At least four graphs can fit on one page, and more than one item may be tracked per graph. Once the reporting has gone through the shakedown to get preliminary errors corrected, you may decide to publish and circulate the results weekly or monthly. Expect two or three months "incubation time" before there will be evidence of a "knee" in the curves, showing that the program is starting to deliver real benefits. Sometimes numbers get worse for a short time when quality improvement is an initial focus. Your plant needs to know these startup difficulties might occur, but that the improvements will come and will make a dramatic positive difference.

In selecting which metrics to use in your operation, we suggest:

1. Use as many as possible from whatever metrics you are currently using and consider important for your business, even if these differ somewhat from the recommendations above.

2. Pick relevant ones which represent known needs or problem areas, or those where management wants to make major improvements.

3. Define the metric so that it is as unaffected by changes in volume or product mix as is possible.

4. Be diplomatic when choosing the measures. For example, do not emphasize labor cost reduction in a plant with a history of poor union-management relations.

5. Where we have suggested "per hundred," decide for yourself whether it might be more appropriate to use "per unit" or "per thousand" in your particular case. Change the metric to suit your situation.

6. Avoid including metrics which people may want to sell (things such as field service, spare parts, or additional software). Inclusion of these might distort results.

7. Meet with key managers at least semiannually to review the metrics and to add, delete, or change them so that they remain as relevant as possible.

Capturing data at the beginning of your efforts and systematically tracking the information will furnish data showing that a measurable benefit can be achieved by application of the rules of process discipline.

In addition to these quantifiable examples which can be graphically represented, anecdotes about successful results ought to be added to the record as well. These "soft" measures often carry more weight with the rank and file simply because they can include emphatic information about the human elements involved. It is also easier to reach consensus on the accuracy of the information. Assuming that you have followed our recommendations regarding communication during the implementation phase, you ought to have many anecdotal references gleaned from newsletters, bulletin boards, and so on.

Our assertion that process discipline affords its adherents a competitive advantage in the marketplace brings another possibility for measuring successful implementation: Many industries regularly benchmark themselves through objective external audit. If you participate in such surveys, and the survey includes process-related performance measures, then you should be able to clearly identify your organization's improvement compared to those you benchmark. The timeline should confirm that implementation of process discipline made the difference.

We often observe that after plants have experienced many months of working under stringent process discipline, the very absence of measurable problems can itself become a problem. There is a tendency to relax the rules and overlook some lapses in discipline. Just as cracks tend to propagate until there is a fracture, so too with complacency regarding process discipline. Audits provide an ongoing measure of the state of process discipline. If discrepancies trend upward or corrective action slackens, then it is time to reinforce your efforts to achieve near-perfect consistency.

Example: A Manufacturing Manager's Day at Work in a Process Discipline Environment

We can explain the components of process discipline, provide some specific examples, and offer a few sample forms, and we have tried to do so throughout this book. It is perfectly clear to us how all of this comes together to create and nourish an environment of process discipline. Further, we know deeply and completely how superior this environment is to alternative ways of operating a manufacturing facility.

For our readers, though, all of this may be less than obvious. Let us follow a day in the life of a champion of process discipline who also happens to be a manager of manufacturing at a medium-sized factory perhaps not so different from yours. This is a fictitious example, and all of the names of the characters in this small script are also fictitious. The events are a composite of many scenes played out in factories with which we are familiar. We have compressed the events into a single day, and have done our best to make them generic enough so that they encompass the flavor of a plant midway in its journey to establish process discipline.

7:20 A.M.—Another Day at Springfield Plant Begins

Ed Evans wheels his late-model Bronco up to the gate, inserts his badge access card into the reader, and cheerfully shouts "Good morning, Janet," to the security guard who flashes him a big grin and nods in acknowledgement to the manufacturing manager as his vehicle passes her booth.

It is Monday and Ed is painfully aware that there is a lot to accomplish this week: the quarterly review is scheduled for Thursday and Friday; that means the corporate vice president will be flying in. The final-finish department head has asked for a meeting today at 3:00 P.M. to prepare a team of shop floor employees for a visit to an important customer who is experiencing some problems with the 6340 product. The first pass at the capital budget is due this week. And there are the usual meetings, decisions, judgment calls and negotiating — the union contract is coming up for renewal this year, so both sides are extraordinarily sensitive to implications in every interaction.

7:30 — Prepping the Day

In quick succession, Ed picks up the weekend report from the hanging rack below the window on his door, flips on the light in his office, and settles into his desk chair. Scanning the report, he is pleased to see that it has been a pretty quiet weekend: only two emergency changes submitted, and the audits conducted by the weekend support team show few discrepancies. He writes a few brief words of praise and encouragement on the front of the report and puts it in his out basket for delivery to the weekend team leader (a rotating position).

A few short months ago, when he had first suggested that the skeleton management team responsible for plant operations during the weekend — the "Weekend Warriors" — conduct the daily audit and ensure discrepancies are addressed before leaving the plant, more than a few people had grumbled about the extra duties. Now, even the skeptics agree that the audit helps the team focus their activities, reduces the time the Warriors have to spend in the plant, and nips most problems in the bud. There have been several consecutive weeks without a single problem call-in. Everyone agrees that is a real advantage — and almost everyone agrees that the focus on operating to standard has been long overdue.

Prior to Ed's tenure, an "anything goes as long as the product gets made" attitude predominated on weekends, and the result was frequent calls to the Warriors to assist with problem solving when equipment and processes went awry. Not unexpectedly, statistics on returned product showed a disproportionate amount of these returns had manufacturing dates traceable to weekends.

Data are not available yet to confirm that these statistics are improving, primarily because there is a long time constant between shipping and feedback from the field. Nonetheless, Ed is absolutely confident that he will be able to demonstrate how effective the weekend audit program is. He used the same technique when he was at Woodhull, and there the statistics (compiled before he started process discipline, then again 18 months later) had clearly shown not only a dramatic reduction in returned product, but also that a return was no more likely to occur on a weekend or off-shift than at any other time.

The flashing message on his telephone alerts him to waiting voice mail. There are six messages; the last of them a long message from one of the maintenance managers, complaining that the production schedule has again disallowed Friday's scheduled preventive maintenance (PM) on the outgas furnace. Jack Crounce's husky voice ends with a sigh, then this: "If you guys aren't serious about this PM stuff, just let me know and I'll stop trying to meet the schedule it took us six weeks to put together!" Ed decides to loop through the maintenance department during his morning walkabout to see if Jack is in a better mood this morning. He jots a brief note to himself so that he will remember to bring up PM during this morning's production meeting.

8:00 — Walkabout

No coffee yet this morning, since he's trying to cut back from his usual six or seven cups a day. Still, he relishes the rich aroma drifting out from the conference area where the chemical processing department is beginning a hazardous materials training session for off-shift personnel. He has offered to open this meeting for David Chen, the department head.

"You guys are going about this exactly right," he tells the 20 or so people sitting before him. "I'm proud of you. It isn't easy for some of you to be here after you've worked all night, and *almost* all of you look wide awake," he tells them, surveying the room. "I told David I wanted to be here to thank you for the work you did to review the new documents and ensure that the safety section of all 35 of them is current, accurate, and appropriate. I'm going to ask each of you to make sure they stay that way."

"Say, Ed," says the voice belonging to the hand which suddenly shoots up at the back of the room. "What I want to know is, are we going to get a pay increase now that we're having to do all this reading and writing in addition to our regular jobs?" Smitty is a good worker, Ed knows, but he is also something of an instigator. He has taken some college courses using the plant's education reimbursement program, and there is seldom a meeting where he passes up an opportunity to state an opinion or ask a sardonic question. Clearly, he enjoys putting management on the spot.

"Smitty, the reason we're asking you guys to help with this is because it's pretty clear that you know a whole lot more about what ought to go in those documents than I do." Ed makes solid eye contact with his harasser, lets the chuckles die down, then breaks into a broad grin. "I expect you and the factory come out about even on this. You and your co-workers get a safe environment to work in and also a say-so in helping us keep it safe. If you want to talk some more, give Kathy a call and set something up on my calendar, OK?" Ed knows how important it is to reinforce the work that has been done. He also wants to convey his own dedication to keeping process discipline alive.

"Thanks, David, for giving me a chance to say hello and thank you guys," he says as he leaves the room. He makes a mental note to talk with David about Smitty — there is a vacancy on the plant's safety committee and Smitty clearly has the energy and intelligence to make a real contribution. Maybe with a little encouragement and attention Smitty can be coaxed into offering his services.

As he approaches the furnace area, Suzie Trang stops him in the aisle. "Hey, Ed, thanks for helping us resolve that calibration issue," she tells him. "I always knew that gauge was unreliable, but it wasn't until we added it to our audit that I could prove how often it drifts out of calibration. The new schedule has solved the problem, and I feel a lot better now."

While he knew he couldn't take full credit for her remark, Ed did take particular pride in the new calibration laboratory. It was part of his plan to bring process discipline to this factory — the fourth factory he had worked in during his 16-year career.

Jason McEnroe, the furnace department head, snaps him a mock salute as they approach each other from opposite ends of the aisle. "Hey, Ed, are all the dogs and ponies ready for the show on Thursday?" "Yeah, pretty much so, I guess," Ed smiles back as they draw up to each other and each pauses.

"Is it OK, then, if I bring up a couple of other issues in this morning's meeting? We need to have equipment engineering get cracking on that document for the new furnace. They still haven't got it finished, and we aren't going to turn that sucker on until our folks are trained. Remember the last time?"

Yes, Ed does remember the last time. Shortly after he came onboard at Springfield, one of the off-shift crew had inadvertently caused a "train wreck" and thousands of dollars of product and equipment had been ruined by the catastrophe. As if that wasn't bad enough, two critical customer shipments had been missed due to lack of product. The customer filled in with a competitor's product, and it had taken some serious negotiation to smooth things over. "Sure, Jason, bring it up. It's important." Ed says as he returns a mock salute and moves back into the aisle to resume his walkabout.

Too bad Jack Crounce is not in his office as Ed swings through the maintenance shop. Well, at least I can show him support during this morning's meeting, Ed thinks to himself.

As he loops his way around the factory, he stops often to check a logbook or examine the blue paperwork that signals an experiment in progress. People wave or smile as he moves through their area. When he first arrived here at Springfield, some people reacted suspiciously when they saw him on the shop floor. Now they expected him and commented if he missed a day. It gave them an informal way to bring up topics or make a suggestion. And he listened carefully to what he heard, often bouncing it back to his direct reports for confirmation, suggestions, or action. It is how he keeps his finger on the pulse of the plant — not the only way, but it suits his particular style of management.

9:00 — Production Meeting

The production meeting begins with reports from each of the manufacturing departments. Since it is Monday, each report includes the weekend numbers as well. The two emergency changes are discussed. Next on the agenda are upcoming experiments, and one of these in particular causes heated discussion.

"I know what you are saying, Ajay, but I'm not so sure you are going to be able to come back up as easily as you say you can. You're talking about some pretty major changes to our setup and we've been burned before." The department head is clearly nervous about a major experiment scheduled to start on Friday at the end of the day and continue through the weekend. The experiment plan lacks some important information, as well as engineering coverage for the off-shift. A separate meeting is scheduled to continue the discussion so that the production meeting stays on track. Ed asks to be invited. He does not enjoy playing referee, but he wants to reinforce his commitment to well-planned experiments.

After other agenda items have been cleared, Ed brings up the preventive maintenance schedule. He cites the statistics: three out of 17 schedules have been missed. He relates his disappointment, and asks for explanations. "Ed, you know as well as I do," Tommy Cruz leans forward in his chair and rests both burly forearms on the table. "I would have missed my numbers by a long shot if I had shut that furnace down as scheduled. And I know I'm one of the culprits. I just don't know which you think is more important — that damned PM or getting some product through this place."

Sometimes Ed thinks he should have taken up a different career — something easier, like hostage negotiation maybe. "Tommy," Ed begins, then pauses to reinforce the gravity of what he is about to say, "I want the PM schedule met 100% of the time. I will trade the shortfall in meeting output for the PM schedule," Ed pauses and lets out a slow breath before continuing, "because I know that we will all be better off in the long run. Is that clear?"

The room falls silent. Ed looks around at the faces of these people who do not uniformly accept the reality of process discipline. There is still a lot of work to be done here. Woodhull was like this, too, at first. Later he will stop by Tommy's office and work with him on adjusting the master schedule to take into account the lost time for PM. Maybe he will show him the downtime improvement charts from Woodhull, collected after they implemented maintenance management. Maybe it would be a good idea to send Tommy over to Woodhull for a few days to benchmark that program.

Jason McEnroe breaks the tension by asking about the training for the new furnace, following up on his earlier conversation with Ed. Equipment engineering confirms that the document is scheduled to be finished by Wednesday. Ed congratulates them on getting it done, even though it is a week behind schedule. Jason nods in appreciation, and promises to make his people available as soon as the training can be coordinated through the lead engineer on the project.

After a few more minutes of general discussion, the meeting breaks up and Ed heads back to his office.

10:00 — An Hour With the Plant Manager

Kathy, Ed's administrative support person, is talking on the telephone as Ed approaches her desk. She holds up her hand as a stop sign so that Ed knows she needs his attention. "OK, Jackie, I'll let him know," she says into the receiver. "Ed, you're wanted right away in Terry's office. And it sounds like he is upset."

Terry and Ed had worked together at another facility where they were both department managers. A year ago Terry had been promoted to plant manager here at Springfield, and shortly thereafter Ed had been tapped as manufacturing manager. Springfield's performance had come under close scrutiny and there was serious speculation that if the numbers did not improve fairly quickly, this plant might not remain open. Once a flagship operation, Springfield was now barely holding on to its share of the market, and the competitors were beating them up on price.

When Terry sounds upset, Ed knows from experience that it is serious. He drops his production journal on his desk, takes up a blank pad of lined paper, and heads down the hall to Terry's office.

Terry glances up as Ed knocks on the jamb of the door. "Well, Ed, this really rips me up! Look at this fax from Japan. They are still complaining about our 'careless mistakes.' I thought the process discipline program was supposed to take care of this. Here it is, six months into the mission, and I'm STILL getting this kind of complaint from the field. What gives?"

Ed knows what he has to convey. He has the details. The daily audit results are showing there are still some problems in final packaging and in shipping. Improvement seems to be slower in those departments. The handful of people in those departments have been through process discipline training with their managers, but a few diehards have resisted the message. They view process discipline as a serious encroachment on their "right" to perform their work "their own way."

This discussion with Terry does not go as smoothly as Ed would have liked. One thing is clear, however: the "careless mistakes" have got to stop — and it is his responsibility to make that happen. As he leaves Terry's office, Ed tries to think of a new approach. In the end, he may have to simply make some personnel moves. He will ask Kathy to schedule some time with the human resources manager to involve him in the strategy for bringing about the necessary changes.

11:00 — Phone Calls and Follow-ups

During the next hour, Ed makes a number of phone calls in response to Kathy's stack of yellow while-you-were-out forms. He walks back out to the maintenance department to check with Jack Crounce. It is important to him that Jack understands his viewpoint on PMs. He wants to make sure that Jack is comfortable with the strong stance taken in the morning meeting. Jack is in the process of telling one of the lathe operators all about the meeting.

Back in his office, there are still more calls to return. The hour goes by quickly and his stomach begins to rumble. "Not enough coffee," he thinks to himself.

Noon — Change Control

Pushing his tray along the cafeteria line, Ed eyes the steaming vegetables and decides to go with the daily special. Ruthie hands him the plate and he sets it down beside the napkin-wrapped utensils. He picks up a carton of milk and looks around. Spotting Robin and Carlos just sitting down, Ed carries his tray over to join them.

"Have you worked out the new change control form yet?" Ed asks as he takes a seat opposite Robin.

Robin is currently leading a cross-functional team to improve the process document change form, including making it available electronically on workstations across the plant. Ed participated in setting up the team's charter, and takes advantage of this opportunity to discuss progress with Robin. As they eat their lunch, the three of them talk about ways to involve more people, proof out the proposed new form (Carlos volunteers his department), and the need for more computer access on the manufacturing floor.

Ed suggests that it is certainly possible to set up an electronic notification of changes, once they are approved, through the electronic mail system. Robin agrees to pursue this with one of his friends who works in the information technology (I.T.) department.

Ed makes a mental note to ask Kathy to set up an appointment with the I.T. department head so that they can include additional manufacturing workstations in next year's budget. He will also try to remember to ask him to be sure to support Robin's efforts to figure out a way to get change notification online.

1:00 P.M.– Planning the Presentation

Thursday and Friday's review is going to be hectic. Ed knows he has a terrific story to tell, and he is going to have quite a bit of help in telling it. The department heads will review their progress-to-plan on the heavy documentation schedule to which they have committed. Most have made excellent headway.

He knows Susan Strang, the quality assurance manager, plans to highlight the change control program. He has asked her to tie her presentation in with his graphs showing the progress the plant is making in documenting process changes based on results from well-conducted experiments.

He drafts out several sheets of notes, knowing that Kathy will turn them into a finished product by Thursday morning. She has scheduled a Wednesday afternoon dress rehearsal for all presenters so that he can check for consistency and tone among them all.

2:00 – Coaching With Andrea Stockholtz, the Newest Production Team Leader

"Come on in, Andrea," Ed says as he gestures toward a chair. "How's it going?" he asks. Her brow furrows, and she lowers her eyes to the carpet. "To tell you the truth, Ed, I'm thinking maybe this job is harder than I thought it was going to be. My people seem to want to do a good job, but sometimes I think they spend more time in meetings and training sessions than they do on the floor. A lot of them don't like being off the floor that much. I'm not so sure it's a good thing, either, when we could be making product." She looks up expectantly.

Ed has thought through this particular topic many times. He earned his manufacturing credentials under a command-and-control authoritarian plant manager who believed that if people were not at their work stations, visibly engaged in manipulating control panels and checking product with micrometers and loupes they carried in their shirt pockets, then it was darned likely they were slacking off on the job. He knows there is a better way — a much better way — to run a manufacturing plant.

Coaching a new generation of college-trained team leaders is part of what he loves about his job. Andrea has the right attributes to succeed here, and Springfield needs thoughtful, effective people like her. His job is to help her understand the tools she has available, and how to apply them. Process discipline is the core of this coaching. He talks her through the philosophy of consistency in manufacturing as the mainstay of both day-to-day operations and process improvement, even using his framed copy of the manufacturing process improvement flow chart to illustrate his points.

"And, of course, Andrea," he tells her in summary, "all of the effort we put into documentation, training, audits, and the like pays off in reduced problems and higher product quality, though it is sometimes hard to make a direct correlation. I believe in process discipline because it has worked every single time I've put it into practice."

Later, Ed asks Kathy to put in a call to corporate to see if there is an opening in an upcoming manufacturing improvement workshop. Once there is a hard-core cadre of believers in process discipline here at Springfield, he will work to convince the human resources department to sponsor an on-site program.

3:00 — Prepping the Travel Crew

Finally, a cup of coffee! The deal he made with himself is that he can have all the coffee he wants after lunch. This is his first cup today, and it is especially delicious. The four others around the table are opening their notepads and folders.

"Hey, we're pretty excited about this opportunity," Janelle begins. "I guess I've been elected the ringleader here, Ed, so let's get started."

After a spirited discussion, the plan is laid out. Janelle and her colleagues will fly to Jackson City; their counterparts at the customer's plant will pick them up, join them for dinner, and then drop them at their motel. That will save the company some money, and it will give them a chance to get acquainted before they start work on the following day.

Before they leave for Jackson City, they will meet again to review all of their process documentation. They plan to take a complete set along with them as reference in case questions come up. The 6340 product has a particularly difficult specification. The quality problems have persisted ever since the first runs were made two years ago. Lately there has been some improvement, but not enough. The documents detail the manufacturing process, and audits show the operators are following them. Maybe this visit will uncover something not yet understood. Janelle will be responsible for reporting back after the visit.

This is the first time a team of production operators has visited a customer. He is quite comfortable with Janelle leading the visit. She showed a remarkable affinity for the elements of process discipline, and organized her department's writing program. He trusts her and knows she will represent the plant well.

4:00 — Preparation for the Rest of the Week

By pre-arrangement, this last hour of the workday on Mondays is set aside for Kathy and Ed to work together. They talk about the upcoming review, and Ed goes over his notes so that she can prepare his report. Kathy has pulled up last year's budget and highlighted year-to-date numbers that are overspent. Ed shoves the report into his briefcase, along with the stack of reports, old operation sheets, and other information Kathy has collected for him. He has agreed to write a process document for one of the simpler operations in the plant. It is just one more way he can demonstrate his commitment to process discipline.

5:00 — Leaving the Plant

Ed seldom leaves the plant this early. However, tonight there is a retirement dinner at a local restaurant and he wants to spend at least an hour with his family before the dinner. The guest of honor has 25 years service with the Springfield plant. He was hired in as a shift supervisor when the plant was only a few years old. He has an outstanding attendance record, and through the years he has won numerous awards for dedication and initiative. He helped the plant recover from a serious fire about 15 years ago, working 36 straight hours to muck out the mess. He has been a valuable employee.

Ed is going to deliver the thank you speech and present some special mementos. Most of the people who will be there tonight, including the plant manager, know that Ed is responsible for this retirement. He and the honoree had a good long talk, but they could not reach an agreement. Ed insists that Springfield will run under process discipline, and the guest of honor hates the rigor and the rules. Sometimes it comes down to a parting of the ways.

As he maneuvers the Bronco out of the parking lot and onto the highway, Ed mulls over his day. You win some, you lose some, he thinks to himself. And almost every evening on the drive home he thinks about what Springfield will be like when process discipline is firmly entrenched. It is this vision of the future, and the knowledge of the progress they are making toward that goal, which fuels him.

Retrospective — Why It Works and How We Know It

How do we know that process discipline really works?

A. History

The record of process discipline is that each time it has been implemented with competence and some patience, it has had a major enhancing effect on yields, quality, and cost. The implementing organization can affect how the improvement is allocated among those three, but there has always been a significant benefit.

Process discipline is not like the "Hawthorne Effect," where operations always improved a limited amount when they received management attention and scrutiny; process discipline takes a certain amount of incubation time (typically two months) with little change in results, followed by a long steady climb which goes on for years. The "stories" in the "benefits" discussion all refer to true situations. Every process and plant situation is different, but one improved at 3% a month in yield for 18 months, one went from 55% to 88% yield in 11 months, and one went from mid-40s to mid-80s in 18 months.

All the plant anecdotes in this book are factual, and the quantitative benefits are fairly described. Dozens of others, not specifically mentioned, back them up with similar results.

B. Common Sense

The historical record is one "proof" of the efficacy of process discipline. A different perspective is provided by considering how the basic elements of process discipline work.

Best-Known Method

The development of consensus on the way that an operation should be run is the precursor to documentation. As noted, it involves tapping the experience and ideas of all potential contributors — operators, production supervisors, engineers, maintenance and quality people, individuals with important prior association with the process including R&D scientists, and application engineers representing customer needs. In addition, the review includes study of experiment reports, recent process data, and records of maintenance, tooling, and raw materials.

The trouble-shooting guide encompasses the knowledge and experience of all contributors. The operating procedure, as written, incorporates the total corporate body of knowledge of the process — the best-known method — and that forms the base for training and for auditing. This definition of the process provides the best opportunity for successful operation.

Consistency

The originator of the scientific method, Francis Bacon (1561–1626) said "Truth will sooner come out from error than confusion." If you run a consistent, singular process and it has a weakness, you have a much better chance of finding and fixing the problem than if you are running a variable parallel set of processes, some of which have imperfections. We follow Bacon's guidance because it has proven to be correct over nearly four centuries, and because it resonates with our common sense.

We have seen that consistency applied to the manufacturing process reduces variability, which immediately eliminates some problems and prevents others from occurring. Equally important, it provides the process with the quiescent background and high signal-to-noise ratio which allows it to be improved much faster and more easily (just as Bacon said.)

Predictability, Child of Consistency

You have observed that running a consistent, low variability process makes the predictability of production output much better, and enables you to make and meet customer commitments with more security. What we have not mentioned is the positive impact that consistency-based predictability has on the whole range of forecasts, budgets, capital budgets, advertising and sales planning, and strategic plans. The entire gamut of financial and marketing and operational and R&D integration with manufacturing works as it is supposed to. This enables the business to run rationally. Anyone who has ever had a magazine advertising campaign come out for a product they were not yet ready to deliver, or who has had to go to the board of directors to explain why the capital which was invested in bricks and mortar would not be utilized for at least two more quarters, can appreciate these benefits.

Ideas From Everyone

One of the basic tenets of process discipline is that ideas are welcome from everyone, and, wherever the idea seems feasible, an experimental opportunity is made available. If the idea originator is not able to devise appropriate experiments to prove the idea's viability, skilled assistance is provided. The concept must demonstrate the benefits expected, and it must be shown that there are no adverse side effects, *but these are the same hurdles the plant manager's and the company president's ideas must clear.*

Process discipline recognizes the criticality of openness to new ideas, and the importance of the organization having a bias in favor of new learning. The implementers of process discipline must always be sure that the "discipline" part is not allowed to block learning and changing, but is only used to filter out those proposals that fail to achieve their goals, or introduce new problems.

When process discipline is implemented correctly, process evolution proceeds at a faster pace than in traditional plants, because time and energy are not wasted on bad changes, their diagnoses, and correction. Furthermore, the stability that avoidance of bad changes imparts, builds confidence in the manufacturing organization with both internal and external customers.

C. Science

Process discipline makes use of data-based decision-making, statistically designed experiments, SPC, consistent process, documentation, training to the documents, audits, and control of change. It requires critical review of change proposals and of experiment plans to assure that the testing touches all bases, and that the logic of the suggested proofs holds water. Process discipline tries to make full use of all the scientific techniques available to manufacturing. Its aim is to apply scientific rigor to production actions.

D. Performance Results

Breadth of Performance Gains

Process discipline has been put to the test in many ways. In addition to North America, process discipline has worked effectively in Europe, Asia, South America, and Australia. It has succeeded on automated and manual processes, in new and old plants, on new plant startups and on transfers, in developing and established processes, on discrete parts and continuous streams, and under a variety of political, economic, and cultural environments.

Intrinsic Continuous Improvement and Ever-Increasing Benefits

The manufacturing process improvement flow chart provides a list of actions and a sequence for most efficient process improvement using process discipline as the primary tool. However, when one nears the bottom of column three, process capability improvement, it is already time to start over from the beginning.

The first time around, you concentrated on accomplishing the obvious major things that needed to be fixed or added or diagnosed. When you start over at the top of column one, you have a process operating much less variably, and you can identify many of the next lower-level problems. Those could not be discerned amid the process noise, or were omitted originally so you could focus on the major issues.

Those starting major issues are now behind you, but there are other important ones to work on, and in the same efficient sequence. If you keep cycling through the flow chart, the yields, costs, and product quality become better and better. Your profit margins and competitive advantage keep increasing. Your manufacturing reaches the position of domination. If your product design and your sales/marketing are at least equivalent to the competition's, you should expect to dominate the business. If not, you have those new areas for the application of process discipline.

We authors have seen domination achieved in major businesses — billion-dollar businesses — exactly this way. Now you too can do it.

GLOSSARY

Audit – An independent, systematic check of the operation of the manufacturing process compared with the process documentation. The focus is on settings, measures of process output variables, and whether all techniques and controls specified are being implemented.

Column 1, 2, 3 – References to the columns (with the leftmost column being designated "Column 1") of the manufacturing process improvement flow chart.

Cpk, Cp – Metrics which indicate how many spreads of a given process variable's distribution will fit into that variable's tolerance band. Higher numbers are better than lower numbers. (More detail is available in the note at the end of the glossary.)

Cusum – A method of charting the historical data of an output variable in order to identify when an important change occurred.

Cycle Rate – The production rate of a manufacturing operation when running to standard operating procedure. It is not factored down for startup, job changeover, or maintenance delays.

Downtime – Time scheduled for production, but which cannot be used to manufacture product, usually because of equipment problems, lack of necessary materials, or unavailability of operator.

Kanban – The Japanese word for "sign" or "placcard." Kanbans are used in assembly line operations to signal when parts are needed.

MSDS – Material Safety Data Sheet. A federally required document which details the characteristics, protections, antidotes, storage and handling requirements, etc. for materials designated as "hazardous" under federal statutes.

Multiplied (Overall)Yield – The number of good parts completed through the entire process as a percent of all those parts started.

PDC – Process Document Change. A form used to *propose* a change to the manufacturing process. When appropriate approvals have been gained, the PDC is implemented and incorporated into the applicable documentation.

Percent of Possible – The number of good parts completed through the process as a percentage of those that could have been made if the process ran at 100% yield, 100% uptime (zero downtime), and ran at the SOP rate (cycle rate).

Percent of Standard – The number of good parts completed through the process as a percent of those which were predicted (based on experience, negotiation, or other means) to be completed. Budgets are often set based on this number. *Percent of standard* represents what is *expected* of the process rather than what the process is *capable of delivering*.

Percent Yield – The number of acceptable parts passed on through a given process step as a percentage of the total number of parts which enter the process step.

SOP – Standard Operating Procedure. In this book, SOP refers to a document that details the best-known method for operating the process.

SPC – Statistical Process Control. A collection of statistical techniques used to find the source (root cause) of manufacturing problems and to maintain the process in a state of control. SPC charts are the most important of these techniques. The Western Electric Handbook describes the application of SPC.

Warpage – A measure of a part's maximum deviation from perfect flatness.

Note on Cpk and Cp

Cpk and Cp are metrics which relate a given variable's tolerance band (the numerator) to the actual spread of the distribution of that variable (the denominator).

The simple metric Cp assumes the spread is centered on the tolerance band, so it is biased optimistically (and therefore rarely used).

The metric Cpk includes assumptions about the distribution of the centrality of the variable (within the tolerance band). Two facts to remember about Cpk are:

1. Cpk is a direct function of the tolerance — if the tolerance doubles, then the Cpk doubles as well.

2. Historical data on centrality of a variable are not accurate predictors of what *will be* and certainly not of what *can be* (with vigorous emphasis on running centered on the middle of the tolerance band).

A Cpk of one implies that the three-sigma distribution of the variable (as centered) just fits within the tolerance band. Higher (larger) Cpk values are "better" or "safer."

The combination of tolerance and Cpk can be the subject of negotiation: "If we can increase the tolerance, we can guarantee a higher Cpk."

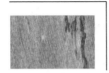

INDEX

Process training, 60-62
  ancillary benefits of, 60-61
  best-known way of operating
    and, 44, 61, 197-198
  nature of, 60
  triggering, 61-62
Product audits, 68, 71
Production information systems,
    112, 139-148
  downtime reporting, 143, 144
  losses by defect and, 142
  material balance, 142-143
  production report in, 139, 140-
    142, 144-148
  rate data, 144-145
  unaccounted for material, 143
  work in process (WIP), 140-141,
    143, 145
Production meetings, 148, 189-191
Production reports, 14
  accounting standards for, 140
  elements of, 140-142
  example, 146-147
  lack of, 148
  materials in, 142-143
  rate information in, 144-145
Product specifications, 31
Profitability, 113-116
Project reviews, 176

QS-9000, 155, 161
Quality control, 158-159
  continuous improvement in, 200
  Good Manufacturing Practices
    (GMP), 119, 161
  parts per million (ppm) quality
    specifications, 1, 159
  process discipline impact on,
    116-118
  safety versus, 179-180
  standards in, 155, 161

statistical process control (SPC)
  in, 16, 18, 19, 20, 112, 139,
    158, 159-161, 199
total quality management
  (TQM), 1, 16-17, 167

Rand Corporation, 127
Randomizing
  of audits, 69
  in experimental design, 85
Ranges, 71, 160-161
Recidivism, 113, 169
Redlining changes, 76
Reports
  audit, 69-71
  downtime, 143, 144, 150, 169
  experiment, 89-94
  production, 139, 140-142, 144-
    148
  See also Documentation
Residuals, 96
Resistance reactions
  antidotes to, 165
  types of, 136-137, 163-166
Rework, 31, 167
Risk, data as antidote to, 22-24
Rohm & Haas, 127

Safety
  in equipment specifications, 40,
    43
  for inspection procedures, 54,
    55
  MSDS (Material Safety Data
    Sheet), 34, 35, 48-49
  in process specifications, 48-49,
    51
  quality control versus, 179-180
Sampling, 16
Schedules
  strategic maintenance, 150

Also available from Quality Resources...

Design for Quality: An Introduction to the Best of Taguchi and Western Methods of Statistical Experimental Design
Robert H. Lochner and Joseph E. Matar
250 pp., 1990, Item No. 916331, hardcover

The Process Reengineering Workbook: Practical Steps to Working Faster and Smarter Through Process Improvement
Jerry L. Harbour, Ph.D.
158 pp., 1994, Item No. 762407, spiral

Keeping Score: Using the Right Metrics to Drive World-Class Performance
Mark Graham Brown
224 pp., 1996, Item No 763128, hardcover

The Basics of FMEA
Robin E. McDermott, Michael R. Beauregard, and Raymond J. Mikulak
80 pp., 1996, Item No 763209, paperback

The Basics of Mistake-Proofing
Michael R. Beauregard, Raymond J. Mikulak, and Robin E. McDermott
66 pp., 1997, Item No. 763276, paperback

The Basics of Performance Measurement
Jerry L. Harbour, Ph.D.
80 pp., 1997, Item No 763284, paperback

Process Mastering: How to Establish and Document the Best-Known Way to Do a Job
Ray W. Wilson and Paul Harsin
168 pp., 1998, Item No 763446, paperback

The 5S Pocket Guide
Jim Peterson and Roland Smith, Ph.D.
64 pp., 1998, Item No. 763381, paperback

SPC Simplified: Practical Steps to Quality, 2nd Edition
Robert T. Amsden, Howard E. Butler, and Davida M. Amsden
304 pp., 1998, Item No. 763403, paperback

For additional information on any of the above titles or for our complete catalog, call 1-800-247-8519 or 212-979-8600.
Visit us at www.qualityresources.com
E-mail: info@qualityresources.com
Quality Resources, 902 Broadway, New York, NY 10010